Baker's®
═══ BOOK OF ═══
CHOCOLATE
═══ RICHES ═══

GOLDEN®
Golden Press • New York
Western Publishing Company, Inc.
Racine, Wisconsin

Second Printing, 1985
Copyright © 1983 by General Foods Corporation
All rights reserved. Produced in the U.S.A.
Library of Congress Catalog Card Number: 83-82254
Golden® and Golden Press® are trademarks of Western Publishing Company, Inc.
ISBN 0-307-49272-9

Baker's
BOOK OF
CHOCOLATE
RICHES

GOLDEN

Golden Press • New York

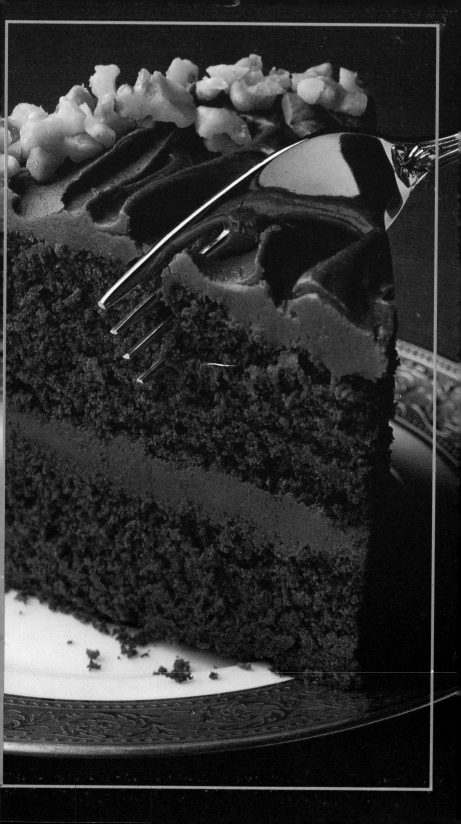

Chocolate... the very word conjures up luscious fantasies, memories of mouth-watering delights. The welcoming chocolate brownies and milk Mom set out as an after-school treat. The fabulous fudge cake that appeared, flaming with candles, on family birthdays. Summer afternoons on Grandmother's porch, with freshly baked chocolate cookies and lemonade. Heavenly chocolate sauce dripping down your favorite ice cream, reward for a particular accomplishment. The melt-in-your-mouth dessert you always ordered in your favorite restaurant.

And Baker's chocolate has always been a part of those delicious memories. For over 200 years we have been producing chocolate, the fine rich baking chocolate that made those memorable desserts. Here we bring you an exciting collection of such recipes—all those special ones you remember, the Old World classics, the all-American favorites, plus some wonderful new ways with that most popular of all ingredients... chocolate.

The cover cake, Wellesley Fudge Cake, goes back to the late 1800's. Two Wellesley College graduates found a recipe for fudge cake in a Boston newspaper and started making it for the Wellesley Tea Room. The cake has been famous ever since. No doubt they used Baker's baking chocolate for its unique richness. Baker's had already been making fine chocolate for over 100 years. Recipe, page 12.

CONTENTS

═══ CHOCOLATE ═══
GIFT FROM THE GODS

The story of chocolate is a uniquely American one, one that goes back to the discovery of the New World. Among the treasures Columbus brought back to King Ferdinand were a few brown beans, probably cocoa beans. No one knew exactly what to do with them until later, when Cortez visited Mexico. There in the court of Montezuma he drank a brew made from such beans. The Aztecs called it "cacahuatl," or "gift from the gods." Cortez brought the chocolate back to Spain and eventually the drink was introduced to the rest of Europe. Soon chocolate houses appeared everywhere, and stopping at one to sip the delicious drink and gossip became part of the social routine.

In this country, the colonists imported their chocolate, but it was an expensive treat. Then in 1765 an Irish immigrant, John Hannon, started milling chocolate in Dorchester, Massachusetts. The price went down and chocolate became a popular drink. The popularity increased enormously after the Boston Tea Party in 1773, when patriots started boycotting tea, and drinking chocolate became an attractive alternative. And that brings us to the second part of the chocolate story…

The Baker's Chocolate Story

When John Hannon started that first mill in Dorchester, he was encouraged and helped financially by Dr. James Baker, a young Harvard graduate who had started his own country store there. Subsequently, in 1780, after Hannon had been lost at sea, Dr. Baker took over the mill. It became a family enterprise, operating as Baker and Son from 1791 to 1804, with James' son Edmund as partner. In 1818 Edmund's son Walter joined as partner, and after Edmund's retirement in 1824 the company became the Walter Baker company.

It has been said that the story of this firm is, in miniature, the story of American business. Walter Baker was an aggressive businessman, and a stickler for quality. In a message to agents he instructed them to return any chocolate products that "are the worse for age." Later, when

Baker's chocolates began to have imitators, he issued this statement: "The stamp 'W. Baker's' on chocolate and cocoa is pure gold anywhere, but as for any other stamp, I can say nothing of consequence."

The company continued to expand and progress, reflecting the history of the country itself. In 1833, Walter Baker's chocolate could be found on the shelves of the store Abraham Lincoln co-owned in Old Salem, Illinois. In 1849 Baker's chocolate went along on the Gold Rush, shipped to San Francisco in individual tin boxes which the miners could use later for gold dust. In 1852 a new kind of chocolate was introduced, Baker's German's sweet chocolate, named for Samuel German, who had come from England, worked as Walter Baker's coachman, then helped perfect this delectable sweet chocolate. With the coming of the Industrial Age, advances were made in the processing; the first chocolate wrapping machines, an electric refrigerating plant. And in 1927, the Baker chocolate company became a division of General Foods.

The high standards established by Walter Baker have continued to the present day. That's why, over the years, American home bakers have learned to rely on the continuing quality of Baker's chocolate, why they look for the Baker's label, with its charming little signature lady. And that leads us to another story...

The Story of La Belle Chocolatiere

It's a fairy-tale story of an Austrian prince and a pretty waitress, and it actually took place in Vienna in the 18th century. He was a dashing prince, presumably handsome; she was of humble, but creditable, origins. One day Prince Dietrichstein came into the Viennese chocolate house where Anna Beltauf worked, was served by the pretty waitress and—so the story goes—immediately fell in love with her. After overcoming all the royal obstacles, they were eventually married. As a wedding gift, the Prince had her portrait painted in her picturesque chocolatiere costume. It was done by a Swiss painter, Jean-Etienne Liotard, and the painting later hung in the Dresden Museum.

Henry Pierce, who had become president of Baker's chocolate following Walter's death, was enchanted with the portrait and determined to use it as a symbol of the company. That was accomplished in 1882, and the little chocolate waitress has been used as a trademark ever since. You'll see her on all Baker's chocolates, and you'll see her throughout this book, symbolizing, as she has for over a century, the finest of cooking chocolates.

CAKES

German Chocolate Cake

1 package (4 oz.) Baker's German's sweet chocolate
½ cup boiling water   2 cups flour
1 teaspoon baking soda   ½ teaspoon salt
1 cup butter or margarine
2 cups sugar   4 egg yolks
1 teaspoon vanilla
1 cup buttermilk   4 egg whites
Coconut-Pecan Filling and Frosting

Melt chocolate in boiling water. Cool. Mix flour, soda and salt. Cream butter and sugar until light and fluffy. Add egg yolks, one at a time, beating thoroughly after each. Blend in vanilla and chocolate. Alternately add flour mixture and buttermilk, beating after each addition until smooth. Beat egg whites until stiff peaks form. Fold into batter.

Pour into three 9-inch layer pans, lined on bottoms with waxed paper. Bake at 350° for 30 to 35 minutes, or until a cake tester inserted in centers comes out clean. Immediately run spatula around pans between cakes and sides. Cool in pans 15 minutes. Remove from pans; remove paper and finishing cooling on racks. Spread filling and frosting between layers and over top.

Coconut-Pecan Filling and Frosting: Combine 1 cup evaporated milk or heavy cream, 1 cup sugar, 3 slightly beaten egg yolks, ½ cup butter or margarine and 1 teaspoon vanilla in saucepan. Cook and stir over medium heat until mixture thickens, about 12 minutes. Remove from heat and stir in 1⅓ cups (about) Baker's Angel Flake coconut and 1 cup chopped pecans. Cool until of spreading consistency, beating occasionally. Makes 2½ cups.

Pictured: Kentucky Jam Cake, page 9; Paisley Chocolate Cake, page 8; German Chocolate Cake, above.

Paisley Chocolate Cake

1⅔ cups flour   1½ cups sugar
2 teaspoons Calumet baking powder
¼ teaspoon baking soda   1 teaspoon salt
½ cup shortening   1 cup evaporated milk
2 eggs   1 teaspoon vanilla
2 squares Baker's semi-sweet or unsweetened
chocolate, melted and cooled
¼ cup evaporated milk
2 squares Baker's semi-sweet or unsweetened
chocolate, melted and cooled
Creamy Mint Frosting

Mix flour, sugar, baking powder, soda and salt. Stir shortening just
to soften. Add flour mixture and 1 cup milk; mix until all flour is
moistened. Beat 2 minutes. Add eggs, vanilla, 2 squares chocolate
and ¼ cup milk. Beat 1 minute longer.

Pour into 2 greased and floured 9-inch layer pans. Pour 2 squares
chocolate in a circle on top of batter in pans about 1 inch from
sides. Swirl chocolate through batter with a spatula, once around
pans. Bake at 350° for 25 to 30 minutes, or until cake tester inserted in centers comes out clean. Cool in pans 10 minutes. Remove
from pans and finish cooling on racks. Spread frosting between
layers and around sides (or use decorating bag and pipe frosting on
sides); leave top unfrosted.

Creamy Mint Frosting: Blend ¾ cup milk into 3 tablespoons flour
in saucepan. Cook and stir until mixture is very thick. Cool. Meanwhile, cream ⅔ cup butter or margarine. Gradually beat in ⅔ cup
sugar and continue beating until light and fluffy. Stir in ⅛ teaspoon peppermint extract and 5 drops green food coloring. Add
flour mixture; beat until creamy and smooth. Makes 2¼ cups.

Kentucky Jam Cake

1½ cups flour   1 teaspoon baking soda
½ teaspoon salt   1 teaspoon allspice
¼ teaspoon cinnamon   ¾ cup buttermilk
2 tablespoons whiskey, bourbon or fruit juice
⅓ cup shortening   ½ cup granulated sugar
½ cup firmly packed brown sugar
3 eggs, separated
½ cup seedless raspberry or blackberry jam
2 squares Baker's unsweetened chocolate,
melted and cooled
1 cup raisins   ½ cup chopped nuts

Mix flour, soda, salt and spices. Combine buttermilk and whiskey. Cream shortening. Gradually beat in sugars and continue beating until light and fluffy. Add egg yolks and beat thoroughly. Alternately add flour and buttermilk mixtures, beating after each addition until smooth. Blend in jam and chocolate. Fold in raisins and nuts. Beat egg whites until stiff peaks form; fold into batter.

Pour into well-greased 9-inch tube pan. Bake at 350° for 50 to 55 minutes, or until cake tester inserted in center of cake comes out clean. Cool in pan 15 minutes. Remove sides of pan and finish cooling upright on rack. Loosen from tube and bottom; invert onto rack. Wrap in aluminum foil or plastic wrap. Store in refrigerator at least 2 days to mellow flavors. Serve at room temperature. Sprinkle with confectioners sugar and garnish with Chocolate Butterflies (page 88) and raspberries, if desired.

Very Berry Chocolate Cake

1 quart fresh strawberries
Chocolate Glaze (page 85)
2 tablespoons sugar
1 teaspoon vanilla
1¾ cups heavy cream*
3 tablespoons sugar*
¾ teaspoon vanilla*
2 baked 9-inch Mahogany Sour Cream Cake (page 13) or
Wellesley Fudge Cake (page 12) layers, cooled

*Or use 3½ cups thawed Cool Whip whipped topping.

Select 5 large strawberries for garnish. Partially dip into glaze and set aside. Hull and halve remaining strawberries. Add 2 tablespoons sugar and 1 teaspoon vanilla; mix gently. Whip cream with 3 tablespoons sugar and ¾ teaspoon vanilla until soft peaks form. Place one cake layer on serving plate; spoon on half of the strawberries. Drizzle with half of the glaze; top with half of the sweetened whipped cream. Repeat layers with remaining ingredients. Garnish with chocolate-dipped strawberries.

Wellesley Fudge Cake

4 squares Baker's unsweetened chocolate
½ cup water   1¾ cups sugar
1⅔ cups flour   1 teaspoon baking soda
1 teaspoon salt   ½ cup butter or margarine
3 eggs   ¾ cup milk
1 teaspoon vanilla
Hungarian Chocolate Frosting (page 80)

Melt chocolate in water in saucepan over very low heat, stirring constantly until smooth. Add ½ cup of the sugar; cook and stir 2 minutes longer. Cool. Mix flour, soda and salt. Cream butter. Gradually beat in remaining 1¼ cups sugar and continue beating until light and fluffy. Add eggs, one at a time, beating thoroughly after each. Alternately add flour mixture and milk, beating after each addition until smooth. Blend in vanilla and chocolate mixture.

Pour into 2 greased and floured 9-inch layer pans. Bake at 350° for 30 to 35 minutes, or until cake tester inserted in centers comes out clean. Cool in pans 10 minutes. Remove from pans and finish cooling on racks. Spread frosting between layers and over top and sides. Garnish with chopped nuts, if desired.

Martha Washington Devil's Food Cake

4 squares Baker's unsweetened chocolate
2 cups sugar   1½ cups buttermilk or sour milk
2 cups flour   1½ teaspoons Calumet baking powder
1 teaspoon baking soda   1 teaspoon salt
¾ cup butter or margarine   3 eggs
1 teaspoon vanilla
Classic Fudge Frosting (page 81)

Melt chocolate in saucepan over very low heat, stirring constantly until smooth. Add ½ cup of the sugar and ½ cup of the buttermilk;

stir until well blended. Cool thoroughly. Mix flour, baking powder, soda and salt. Cream butter. Gradually beat in remaining 1½ cups sugar and continue beating until light and fluffy. Add eggs, one at a time, beating thoroughly after each. Blend in about one-fourth of the flour mixture. Blend in chocolate mixture and vanilla. Alternately add remaining flour mixture and remaining 1 cup buttermilk, beating after each addition until smooth.

Pour into 2 greased and floured 9-inch layer pans. Bake at 350° about 40 minutes, or until cake tester inserted in centers comes out clean. Cool in pans 10 minutes. Remove from pans and finish cooling on racks. Spread frosting between layers and over top and sides.

Mahogany Sour Cream Cake

3 squares Baker's unsweetened chocolate
½ cup water   1 cup (½ pt.) sour cream
1⅓ cups flour   1½ teaspoons Calumet baking powder
1 teaspoon baking soda   1 teaspoon salt
⅔ cup butter or margarine
⅔ cup firmly packed light brown sugar
1 cup granulated sugar   3 eggs
2 teaspoons vanilla   Continental Flair Frosting (page 84)

Melt chocolate in water in saucepan over very low heat, stirring constantly until smooth. Cool; then stir in sour cream. Mix flour, baking powder, soda and salt. Cream butter. Gradually beat in sugars; beat until light and fluffy. Add eggs, one at a time, beating thoroughly after each. Alternately add flour and chocolate mixtures, beating after each addition until smooth. Stir in vanilla.

Pour into 2 well-greased and floured 9-inch layer pans. Bake at 350° for 35 to 40 minutes, or until cake tester inserted in centers comes out clean. Cool in pans 10 minutes. Remove from pans and finish cooling on racks. Spread frosting between layers and over top and sides of cake.

Viennese Chocolate Torte

1 cup flour
½ teaspoon salt
½ cup ground walnuts
¾ cup unsalted butter
1¼ cups confectioners sugar
8 egg yolks
1 package (8 squares) Baker's semi-sweet
chocolate, melted and cooled
1 teaspoon vanilla   8 egg whites
1 cup (10-oz. jar) apricot jam
Continental Flair Frosting (page 84)
Sweetened whipped cream or thawed Cool Whip
whipped topping

Mix flour, salt and walnuts. Cream butter. Gradually beat in sugar and continue beating until light and fluffy. Add egg yolks, a few at a time, beating thoroughly after each addition. Gradually stir in chocolate. Add flour mixture and vanilla, stirring just to blend. Beat egg whites until soft peaks form. Blend about ¼ cup of the beaten egg whites into the chocolate mixture; gently fold in remaining egg whites.

Pour into 2 greased and floured 9-inch layer pans. Bake at 350° for 40 to 45 minutes, or until cake tester inserted in centers comes out clean. Cool in pans 10 minutes. Remove from pans and finish cooling on racks.

Split layers horizontally, making 4 layers. Stir jam in saucepan over low heat until melted. Spread about ⅓ cup over tops of three layers. Stack on a rack placed on a tray; top with fourth layer. Prepare frosting as directed, cooling only slightly. Pour quickly over cake, covering top and sides. Place cake on serving plate. If desired, spoon frosting drippings into plastic-lined decorating bag fitted with writing tip; pipe a name or greeting on cake. Store in refrigerator at least one day to mellow flavors. Serve at room temperature with sweetened whipped cream.

Pictured: Black Forest Cake, page 16; Viennese Chocolate Torte, above.

Black Forest Cake

¼ cup kirsch brandy*
1 can (21 oz.) cherry pie filling, drained
2 baked 9-inch Martha Washington Devil's Food
Cake (page 12) layers, cooled
3 cups heavy cream**   ⅓ cup sugar**
1½ teaspoons vanilla**
Chocolate Curls (page 86)
Chocolate Trees (page 88)

*Or use ½ teaspoon almond extract.
**Or use 6 cups thawed Cool Whip whipped topping.

Stir kirsch into pie filling. Place one cake layer on serving plate.
Spoon pie filling evenly over cake layer. Whip cream with sugar
and vanilla until soft peaks form. Spread about 2 cups evenly over
cherries. Top with second cake layer. Spread remaining whipped
cream over top and sides of cake. Press chocolate curls onto sides of
cake. Garnish top with chocolate trees or additional chocolate
curls. Chill at least 1 hour before serving.

Chocolate Almond Cake l'Orange

6 tablespoons butter or margarine   1 cup sugar
⅛ teaspoon salt   3 eggs
4 squares Baker's unsweetened chocolate, melted and cooled
¾ cup ground almonds   ¼ cup dry bread crumbs
3 tablespoons orange liqueur   1 teaspoon vanilla

Cream butter. Gradually beat in sugar and salt and continue beating until light and fluffy. Add eggs, one at a time, beating thoroughly after each. Stir in chocolate, almonds, bread crumbs,
2 tablespoons of the liqueur and the vanilla.

Pour into greased and floured 8-inch layer pan. Bake at 375° about
25 minutes, or until cake tester inserted in center comes out clean.

Cool in pan 5 minutes. Invert onto rack and drizzle with remaining 1 tablespoon liqueur. Cool. Garnish with sweetened whipped cream and thinly slivered orange rind, if desired.

Chocaroon Cake

3 squares Baker's semi-sweet chocolate
¼ cup water   1 egg white
Dash of salt   ¼ cup sugar
2 tablespoons flour
1⅓ cups (about) Baker's Angel Flake coconut
1¾ cups flour
1½ teaspoons Calumet baking powder
1 teaspoon baking soda   1 teaspoon salt
1 cup (½ pt.) sour cream
½ cup butter or margarine
1 cup sugar   3 eggs
2 teaspoons vanilla
Chocolate Glaze (page 85)

Melt chocolate in water in saucepan over very low heat, stirring constantly until smooth. Cool thoroughly. Beat egg white with dash of salt until foamy throughout. Gradually add ¼ cup sugar and continue beating until mixture forms stiff peaks. Blend in 2 table-spoons flour and the coconut. Mix 1¾ cups flour, the baking powder, soda and 1 teaspoon salt. Stir sour cream into chocolate.

Cream butter. Gradually beat in 1 cup sugar and continue beating until light and fluffy. Add eggs, one at a time, beating thoroughly after each. Blend in vanilla. Alternately add flour and chocolate mixtures, beating after each addition.

Pour about three-fourths of the batter into greased and floured 9-inch tube pan. Spoon coconut mixture in a ring on batter in pan; cover with remaining batter. Bake at 350° about 60 minutes, or until cake tester inserted in center of cake comes out clean. Cool completely in pan on rack; then remove from pan. Top with glaze.

Mocha Spice Cake

1½ cups flour   1 teaspoon baking soda
1 teaspoon cinnamon   ½ teaspoon Calumet baking powder
½ teaspoon salt   1 cup (½ pt.) sour cream   ½ cup water
1 tablespoon Maxwell House or Yuban instant coffee
½ teaspoon vanilla   ½ cup butter or margarine
1½ cups sugar   2 eggs
2 squares Baker's unsweetened chocolate, melted and cooled

Mix flour, soda, cinnamon, baking powder and salt. Combine sour cream, water, coffee and vanilla. Cream butter. Gradually beat in sugar; beat until light and fluffy. Add eggs, one at a time, beating thoroughly after each. Blend in chocolate. Alternately add flour and sour cream mixtures; beat after each addition until smooth.

Pour into greased and floured 13x9-inch pan. Bake at 350° for 30 to 35 minutes, or until cake tester inserted in center comes out clean. Cool in pan 10 minutes. Remove from pan and finish cooling on rack. Sprinkle with confectioners sugar, if desired.

Nut Loaves

2¼ cups flour   1 teaspoon baking soda   1 teaspoon salt
1 cup butter or margarine   2 cups sugar   5 eggs
3 squares Baker's unsweetened chocolate, melted and cooled
1 cup buttermilk or sour milk   2 teaspoons vanilla
1 cup finely chopped nuts   Bittersweet Glaze (page 85)

Mix flour, soda and salt. Cream butter. Gradually beat in sugar; beat until light and fluffy. Add eggs, one at a time, beating after each. Blend in chocolate. Alternately add flour mixture and buttermilk, beating after each addition. Mix in vanilla and nuts.

Pour into 2 greased and floured 9x5-inch loaf pans. Bake at 350° about 60 minutes, or until cake tester inserted in centers comes out clean. Cool 10 minutes; then remove from pans and finish cooling on racks. Top with glaze. Garnish with chopped nuts, if desired.

Ricotta Cheesecake

1 recipe Graham Cracker Crumb Crust (page 35)
1 envelope unflavored gelatin   ¼ cup cold water
4 squares Baker's unsweetened chocolate
¾ cup milk   1 cup sugar
1 container (15 oz.) ricotta cheese
1½ teaspoons vanilla   1 cup heavy cream*
2 tablespoons sugar*   ½ teaspoon vanilla*
Sour Cream Topping

*Or use 2 cups thawed Cool Whip whipped topping.

Press prepared crumbs firmly on bottom and 1 inch up sides of 9-inch springform pan. Bake at 375° for 8 minutes. Cool. Soften gelatin in water. Melt chocolate in milk in saucepan over very low heat, stirring constantly until smooth. Add 1 cup sugar and softened gelatin. Heat and stir until smooth. Cool. Beat cheese until fluffy. Blend in chocolate mixture and 1½ teaspoons vanilla. Whip cream with 2 tablespoons sugar and ½ teaspoon vanilla until soft peaks form. Fold into cheese mixture. Pour into crumb-lined pan. Chill until firm, at least 4 hours. Remove sides of pan. Spread with topping. Garnish with Chocolate Curls (page 86), if desired.

Sour Cream Topping: Combine ½ cup sour cream and ½ cup thawed Cool Whip whipped topping. Makes about 1 cup.

Almond Ricotta Cheesecake: Prepare Ricotta Cheesecake as directed, reducing milk to ½ cup and substituting 3 tablespoons almond liqueur for the 1½ teaspoons vanilla.

Orange Ricotta Cheesecake: Prepare Ricotta Cheesecake as directed, reducing milk to ½ cup and substituting 3 tablespoons orange liqueur for the 1½ teaspoons vanilla.

Mocha Ricotta Cheesecake: Prepare Ricotta Cheesecake as directed, dissolving 2 tablespoons Maxwell House or Yuban instant coffee in chocolate-milk mixture.

German Chocolate Cheesecake

1 recipe Graham Cracker Crumb Crust (page 35)
2 packages (4 oz. each) Baker's German's sweet chocolate
½ cup butter or margarine
3 eggs
1 cup sugar
2 teaspoons vanilla
3 packages (8 oz. each) cream cheese,
at room temperature
¼ cup flour
1 cup (½ pt.) sour cream

Press prepared crumbs firmly on bottom and 1 inch up sides of 9-inch springform pan. Melt chocolate with butter in saucepan over very low heat, stirring constantly until smooth. Remove from heat. Meanwhile, beat eggs thoroughly in small mixer bowl. Gradually beat in sugar and continue beating until thick and light in color. Stir in vanilla. Beat cream cheese until light and fluffy in large mixer bowl. Add egg mixture and blend thoroughly. Stir in flour. Stir sour cream into chocolate; then blend into cheese mixture. Pour into crumb-lined pan. Bake at 350° for 1 hour and 15 minutes. Turn off oven, set door ajar and let cake stand in oven for 1 hour. Finish cooling on rack. Chill about 2 hours. Remove sides of pan just before serving.

Holiday Cake

⅔ cup flour   ½ teaspoon Calumet baking powder
½ teaspoon salt   5 eggs
¾ cup sugar
2 squares Baker's unsweetened chocolate
¼ cup cold water   2 tablespoons sugar
¼ teaspoon baking soda
Mocha Frosting (page 81)

Mix flour, baking powder and salt. Beat eggs in large bowl. Gradually beat in ¾ cup sugar; beat until fluffy and light in color. Gradually fold in flour mixture. Melt chocolate in saucepan over very low heat, stirring constantly until smooth. Immediately add water, 2 tablespoons sugar and the soda. Stir until thick and smooth. Blend quickly into batter.

Pour into 15x10-inch jelly roll pan which has been greased on bottom and sides; then lined on bottom with waxed paper and greased again. Bake at 350° for 18 to 20 minutes, or until cake tester inserted in center comes out clean. Remove from pan, remove paper and finish cooling on rack. Cut into three 10x5-inch pieces. Spread frosting between layers and over top and sides. Garnish with Chocolate Leaves (page 89), if desired.

Yule Log: Prepare Holiday Cake; turn out onto a towel, sprinkled with confectioners sugar, after baking. Remove paper and trim off crisp edges of cake. Starting on short side, roll up cake with towel. Cool on rack. Prepare Chocolate Cheese Frosting. Unroll cake and spread with 1¾ cups frosting. Reroll and place on serving plate. Spread remaining frosting on cake. If desired, garnish with rolled green gumdrops cut in holly-leaf shapes and piped with melted chocolate; add red cinnamon candies.

Chocolate Cheese Frosting: Beat 1 package (3 oz.) cream cheese with ¾ cup confectioners sugar until light and fluffy. Add 1 teaspoon vanilla and 4 squares Baker's semi-sweet chocolate, melted and cooled; blend well. Whip 1½ cups heavy cream until soft peaks form; fold into chocolate mixture. Makes 3¼ cups.

PIES

Chocolate Mousse Pie au Rhum

1½ tablespoons sugar
1 package (8 squares) Baker's semi-sweet chocolate
¼ cup water   8 eggs, separated
⅔ cup sugar   1½ teaspoons vanilla
1 teaspoon rum extract*
Dash of salt
1 cup sweetened whipped cream or thawed
Cool Whip whipped topping
Chocolate-Dipped Fruit Morsels (page 74)

Or use ¼ cup dark rum; or use 2 tablespoons orange liqueur and omit vanilla.

Sprinkle 1½ tablespoons sugar evenly on bottom and sides of well-buttered 9-inch pie pan. Melt chocolate in water in saucepan over very low heat, stirring constantly until smooth. Remove from heat. Beat egg yolks; gradually add ⅔ cup sugar and continue beating until yolks are thick and light in color. Blend in chocolate, vanilla and rum extract.

Beat egg whites and salt until mixture forms stiff peaks. Fold carefully into chocolate mixture, blending well. Measure 4 cups into prepared pie pan. Bake at 350° for 25 to 30 minutes or until puffed and firm. Cool 15 minutes; then chill 1 hour. (Center will fall, forming a shell.)

Meanwhile, chill remaining chocolate mixture about 1½ hours; spoon into chilled shell. Chill at least 3 hours. Before serving, garnish with sweetened whipped cream and chocolate-dipped fruit.

Note: Use clean eggs with no cracks in shells.

Fudge Brownie Pie

1 unbaked 9-inch Pie Shell (page 35)
3 squares Baker's unsweetened chocolate
⅓ cup butter or margarine   3 eggs
1¼ cups sugar   Dash of salt
3 tablespoons light corn syrup
3 tablespoons milk   1 teaspoon vanilla

Prick pie shell thoroughly with fork. Bake at 425° about 10 minutes or until lightly browned. Remove from oven; reduce oven temperature to 350°.

Meanwhile, melt chocolate with butter in saucepan over very low heat, stirring constantly until smooth; cool slightly. Beat eggs well. Add sugar, salt, corn syrup, milk and vanilla. Beat in chocolate; then pour into partially baked pie shell. Bake at 350° for 45 to 50 minutes, or until top puffs and begins to crack. Cool. (Center of pie will fall slightly.) Just before serving, fill center with sweetened whipped cream, if desired.

Sweet Coconut Pie

3 squares Baker's unsweetened chocolate
½ cup butter or margarine
3 eggs, slightly beaten   ¾ cup sugar
½ cup flour
1 teaspoon vanilla
⅔ cup sweetened condensed milk
2⅔ cups (about) Baker's Angel Flake coconut

Melt chocolate with butter in saucepan over very low heat, stirring constantly until smooth. Remove from heat. Stir in eggs, sugar, flour and vanilla. Pour into greased 9-inch pie pan. Combine milk and coconut; spoon over chocolate mixture, leaving ½- to 1-inch border. Bake at 350° for 30 minutes. Cool before serving.

Peppermint Pie

½ cup butter or margarine   ¾ cup sugar
3 squares Baker's unsweetened chocolate, melted and cooled
1 teaspoon vanilla   ½ teaspoon peppermint extract
3 eggs   ½ cup heavy cream*
1 tablespoon sugar*   ¼ teaspoon vanilla*
1 baked 9-inch Pie Shell, cooled (page 35)

*Or use 1 cup thawed Cool Whip whipped topping.

Cream butter; gradually beat in ¾ cup sugar and continue beating
until light and fluffy. Add melted chocolate, 1 teaspoon vanilla and
the peppermint extract. Add eggs, one at a time, beating about
1 minute after each. Whip the cream with 1 tablespoon sugar and
¼ teaspoon vanilla until soft peaks form. Fold into chocolate mixture and spoon into pie shell. Chill at least 4 hours. Garnish with
additional sweetened whipped cream and peppermint candies or
chocolate curls, if desired.

Note: Use clean eggs with no cracks in shells.

Coconut Chocolate Pie

4 squares Baker's semi-sweet chocolate*
¼ cup butter or margarine   1 can (13 oz.) evaporated milk
1⅓ cups (about) Baker's Angel Flake coconut
3 eggs, slightly beaten   ½ cup sugar
1 unbaked 9-inch Pie Shell (page 35)

*Or use 1 package (4 oz.) Baker's German's sweet chocolate.

Melt chocolate with butter in saucepan over very low heat, stirring
constantly until smooth. Remove from heat. Blend in milk,
coconut, eggs and sugar; pour into pie shell. Bake at 400° for
30 minutes. Cool. Top with sweetened whipped cream or ice
cream, if desired.

Chiffon Pie

1 envelope unflavored gelatin
¼ cup cold water
2 squares Baker's unsweetened chocolate
½ cup water
4 eggs, separated
¼ cup sugar
¼ teaspoon salt
1 teaspoon vanilla
½ cup sugar
1 baked 9-inch Graham Cracker Crumb Crust, cooled (page 35)
1 cup sweetened whipped cream or thawed
Cool Whip whipped topping

Soften gelatin in ¼ cup water. Melt chocolate in ½ cup water in saucepan over very low heat, stirring constantly until smooth. Remove from heat; add softened gelatin and stir until dissolved. Beat egg yolks. Gradually add ¼ cup sugar and continue beating until light and fluffy. Blend into chocolate mixture. Blend in salt and vanilla. Cool.

Beat egg whites until foamy throughout. Gradually add ½ cup sugar and continue beating until mixture forms stiff peaks. Fold into chocolate mixture; spoon into crumb crust. Chill until set, about 4 hours. When ready to serve, garnish with sweetened whipped cream and chocolate curls, if desired.

Note: Use clean eggs with no cracks in shells.

Pictured: Black Bottom Pie, page 30: Classic Meringue Pie, page 31: Chiffon Pie, above.

Black Bottom Pie

3 eggs, separated   ⅔ cup sugar
¼ teaspoon salt·   1¾ cups milk
4 squares Baker's unsweetened chocolate
2 teaspoons vanilla
1 baked 9-inch Pie Shell, cooled (page 35)
1 envelope unflavored gelatin
¼ cup cold water   ½ cup sugar
½ cup sweetened whipped cream or thawed
Cool Whip whipped topping

Beat egg yolks slightly; then combine with ⅔ cup sugar and the
salt in saucepan. Add milk. Cook and stir over medium heat until
mixture coats a metal spoon, 12 to 15 minutes. Remove from
heat. Add chocolate and vanilla; stir until chocolate is melted and
mixture is smooth. Measure 1¼ cups into pie shell.

Soften gelatin in water. Add to remaining hot chocolate mixture
and stir until gelatin is dissolved. Cool. Beat egg whites until foamy
throughout. Gradually add ½ cup sugar; continue beating until
mixture forms stiff peaks. Blend in cooled chocolate mixture and
the sweetened whipped cream. Spoon carefully over chocolate layer
in shell. Chill until set, about 3 hours. Garnish with additional
sweetened whipped cream and chocolate curls, if desired.

Note: Use clean eggs with no cracks in shells.

Angel Pie

1 package (4 oz.) Baker's German's sweet chocolate
2 tablespoons water   1 cup heavy cream*
1 tablespoon confectioners sugar*   ½ teaspoon vanilla*
Meringue Nut Shell, baked and cooled

*Or use 2 cups thawed Cool Whip whipped topping.

Melt chocolate in water in saucepan over very low heat, stirring
constantly until smooth. Cool until thickened. Whip cream with

sugar and vanilla until soft peaks form. Blend in melted chocolate. Spoon into Meringue Nut Shell and chill at least 2 hours. Garnish with additional sweetened whipped cream, if desired.

Meringue Nut Shell: Beat 2 egg whites, ⅛ teaspoon salt and ⅛ teaspoon cream of tartar until foamy throughout. Gradually add ½ cup sugar and continue beating until meringue forms stiff peaks. Add ½ teaspoon vanilla and ⅓ cup chopped pecans or walnuts. Spread meringue mixture on bottom and sides of well-greased and lightly floured 7- or 8-inch pie pan. Bake at 250° for 40 minutes; turn off heat and cool at least 1 hour in oven.

Classic Meringue Pie

⅔ cup sugar   ⅓ cup flour
½ teaspoon salt   2¾ cups milk
2 squares Baker's unsweetened chocolate
3 eggs, separated   2 teaspoons butter or margarine
2 teaspoons vanilla
1 baked 9-inch Pie Shell, cooled (page 35)
6 tablespoons sugar

Mix ⅔ cup sugar, the flour and salt in saucepan. Gradually stir in milk; add chocolate. Cook and stir over medium heat until mixture is smooth and thickened; then cook and stir 5 minutes longer. Remove from heat. Beat egg yolks slightly. Stir a small amount of the hot mixture into egg yolks, mixing well. Return to remaining hot mixture in saucepan. Cook 2 minutes longer. Blend in butter and vanilla. Cover surface with plastic wrap and cool 30 minutes without stirring. Pour into pie shell.

Beat egg whites until foamy throughout. Gradually add 6 tablespoons sugar and continue beating until meringue forms stiff peaks. Pile lightly on filling; then spread to edge of pie shell to seal well. Bake at 425° for 8 minutes, or until meringue is lightly browned. Cool to room temperature before serving.

Southern Chocolate Pecan Pie

1 package (4 oz.) Baker's German's sweet chocolate
3 tablespoons butter or margarine
1 teaspoon Maxwell House or Yuban instant coffee
⅓ cup sugar
1 cup light corn syrup
3 eggs, slightly beaten
1 teaspoon vanilla
1 cup coarsely chopped pecans
1 unbaked 9-inch Pie Shell (page 35)
Coffee-Flavored Topping

Melt chocolate with butter in saucepan over very low heat, stirring constantly until smooth. Stir in coffee. Remove from heat. Combine sugar and syrup in saucepan. Bring to a boil over high heat, stirring until sugar is dissolved. Reduce heat and boil gently for 2 minutes, stirring occasionally. Remove from heat; add chocolate mixture. Pour slowly over eggs, stirring constantly. Stir in vanilla and pecans; pour into pie shell. Bake at 375° for 45 to 50 minutes, or until filling is completely puffed across top. Cool. Garnish with Coffee-Flavored Topping and pecan halves, if desired.

Coffee-Flavored Topping: Combine 1 teaspoon Maxwell House or Yuban instant coffee, 1 tablespoon sugar, ¼ teaspoon vanilla and ½ cup heavy cream in small bowl. Beat just until soft peaks form. Makes 1 cup.

German Chocolate Pie

1 unbaked 9-inch Pie Shell (page 35)
⅓ cup butter or margarine
⅓ cup firmly packed brown sugar
⅓ cup chopped pecans
⅓ cup Baker's Angel Flake coconut
1 package (6-serving size) Jell-O brand vanilla flavor
pudding and pie filling
1 package (4 oz.) Baker's German's sweet chocolate,
broken in pieces
2½ cups milk
1 cup sweetened whipped cream or thawed
Cool Whip whipped topping

Prick pie shell thoroughly with fork. Bake at 425° for 5 to 8 minutes, or until shell begins to brown. Remove from oven. Meanwhile, combine butter, brown sugar, pecans and coconut in saucepan. Heat until butter and sugar are melted, stirring occasionally. Spread in bottom of pie shell. Bake at 425° for 5 minutes or until bubbly. Cool.

Combine pie filling mix, chocolate and milk in saucepan. Cook and stir over medium heat until mixture comes to a *full bubbling boil.* Remove from heat; beat to blend, if necessary. Cool 5 minutes, stirring occasionally. Pour over coconut mixture in shell; cover surface with plastic wrap. Chill at least 4 hours. Before serving, remove plastic wrap and garnish pie with sweetened whipped cream. Sprinkle with additional coconut, if desired.

Crumb Crust

1¼ cups fine chocolate wafer, graham cracker,
zwieback or gingersnap crumbs
¼ cup sugar
¼ cup butter or margarine, melted

Combine crumbs and sugar; mix in butter. Press firmly on bottom
and sides of a 9-inch pie pan. For an unbaked crumb crust, chill
1 hour before filling. For a baked crumb crust, bake at 375° for
8 minutes. Cool thoroughly before filling. For ease in serving, dip
pie pan in warm water for a few seconds before cutting.

For 7-inch pie pan, use ¾ cup crumbs, 2 tablespoons sugar and
3 tablespoons melted butter.

For 8-inch pie pan, use 1 cup crumbs, 3 tablespoons sugar and
3 to 4 tablespoons melted butter.

Pie Shell

1¼ cups flour
½ teaspoon salt
½ cup shortening
3 tablespoons (about) cold water

Mix flour and salt in bowl. Lightly cut in shortening with a pastry
blender until mixture resembles coarse meal. Sprinkle in water, a
small amount at a time, mixing lightly with pastry blender or fork
until all particles are moistened and cling together when pastry is
pressed into a ball. Cover with a damp cloth and let stand a few
minutes. Roll pastry thin (less than ⅛ inch) on lightly floured
board. Line a 7-, 8- or 9-inch pie pan with pastry. Trim 1 inch larger
than pan; fold under to form standing rim; flute edge.

For a baked pie shell, prick pastry thoroughly with fork. Bake at
425° for 12 to 15 minutes or until lightly browned. Cool.

COOKIES

Beacon Hill Brownies

1 package (8 squares) Baker's unsweetened chocolate
1 cup butter or margarine   5 eggs
3 cups sugar   1 tablespoon vanilla
1½ cups flour   2 cups coarsely chopped walnuts

Melt chocolate with butter in saucepan over very low heat, stirring constantly until smooth. Cool slightly. Beat eggs, sugar and vanilla in large mixer bowl at high speed 10 minutes. Blend in chocolate at low speed. Add flour, beating just to blend. Stir in walnuts. Spread in greased 13x9-inch pan. Bake at 375° for 35 to 40 minutes. (Do not overbake.) Cool in pan. Cut into squares or bars. Makes 24 to 32.

Mint-Glazed Brownies: Prepare Beacon Hill Brownies as directed. While still warm, place about 2 dozen wafer-thin chocolate-coated after-dinner mints on top of brownies. Return to oven about 3 minutes. Then spread softened mints evenly over brownies.

Nut-Topped Brownies: Prepare Beacon Hill Brownies as directed, reducing walnuts to ½ cup and sprinkling them over batter. Bake and cool. Melt 1 square Baker's unsweetened or semi-sweet chocolate with 1 teaspoon butter or margarine in saucepan over very low heat; then drizzle over brownies. Let stand until chocolate is firm.

Marshmallow-Topped Brownies: Prepare Beacon Hill Brownies as directed. While still hot, scatter 2½ cups miniature marshmallows on top of brownies. Return to oven about 3 minutes. Melt 1 square Baker's unsweetened chocolate with 1 teaspoon butter or margarine in saucepan over very low heat; then drizzle over marshmallows. Cut while still warm.

Pictured: Mint-Glazed Brownies, above; Double-Deck Brownies, page 38; Cream Cheese Brownies, page 38.

Double-Deck Brownies

⅔ cup flour   ½ teaspoon Calumet baking powder
¼ teaspoon salt   2 eggs
1 cup sugar
½ cup butter or margarine, melted and cooled
⅓ cup Baker's Angel Flake coconut
¼ teaspoon almond extract
2 squares Baker's unsweetened chocolate, melted
1 square Baker's semi-sweet chocolate, melted

Mix flour, baking powder and salt. Beat eggs thoroughly. Gradually add sugar and continue beating until light and fluffy. Blend in butter; then stir in flour mixture. Measure ½ cup into small bowl. Stir in coconut and almond extract; set aside. Add unsweetened chocolate to remaining batter; spread in greased 8-inch square pan. Drop coconut batter by teaspoonfuls over chocolate batter. Then spread carefully to form a thin layer. Bake at 350° for 30 to 35 minutes or until lightly browned. Cool in pan. Drizzle with semi-sweet chocolate. Cut into squares or bars. Makes about 20.

Cream Cheese Brownies

1 package (4 oz.) Baker's German's sweet chocolate
5 tablespoons butter or margarine
1 package (3 oz.) cream cheese, at room temperature
¼ cup sugar   3 eggs
1 tablespoon flour   ½ teaspoon vanilla
¾ cup sugar   ½ teaspoon Calumet baking powder
¼ teaspoon salt   ½ cup flour
½ cup coarsely chopped nuts   1 teaspoon vanilla

Melt chocolate with 3 tablespoons of the butter over very low heat, stirring constantly until smooth. Cool. Cream remaining 2 tablespoons butter with the cream cheese until smooth. Gradually add

¼ cup sugar, creaming until light and fluffy. Blend in 1 of the eggs, 1 tablespoon flour and ½ teaspoon vanilla.

Beat remaining 2 eggs until light and fluffy. Gradually beat in ¾ cup sugar and continue beating until thickened. Stir in baking powder, salt and ½ cup flour. Blend in chocolate. Stir in nuts and 1 teaspoon vanilla.

Spread half of the chocolate batter in a greased 8- or 9-inch square pan. Spread cheese mixture over the top. Drop remaining chocolate batter by tablespoonfuls over top. Swirl through batters with a spatula to marble. Bake at 350° for 35 to 40 minutes. Cool in pan. Cut into squares or bars. Makes 16 to 20.

Fudgy Brownies

2 squares Baker's unsweetened chocolate
⅓ cup butter or other shortening
⅔ cup flour   ¼ teaspoon salt
½ teaspoon Calumet baking powder
2 eggs   1 cup sugar
1 teaspoon vanilla   ½ cup chopped nuts*

*Or use ¾ cup Baker's Angel Flake coconut.

Melt chocolate with butter in saucepan over very low heat, stirring constantly until smooth. Remove from heat. Mix flour, salt and baking powder. Beat eggs thoroughly. Gradually beat in sugar. Blend in chocolate mixture and vanilla. Add flour mixture, stir well. Stir in nuts. Spread in greased 8-inch square pan. Bake at 350° for 25 minutes (moist chewy brownies) or about 30 minutes (cake-like brownies). Cool in pan. Cut into squares or bars. Makes about 20.

For Brownie Alaska, bake in 8-inch layer pan which has been greased and lined on bottom with waxed paper. Cool 10 minutes. Remove from pan, remove paper and finish cooling on rack.

Note: Recipe may be doubled. Bake in greased 13x9-inch pan for 25 to 30 minutes.

Chunky Chocolate Cookies

2 cups flour
1 teaspoon baking soda
¾ teaspoon salt
1 cup butter or margarine
¾ cup firmly packed dark brown sugar
½ cup granulated sugar
1 teaspoon vanilla
1 egg
¼ cup sour cream
1 cup coarsely chopped nuts
1 package (8 squares) Baker's semi-sweet
chocolate, coarsely chopped

Mix flour, soda and salt. Cream butter. Gradually beat in sugars
and continue beating until light and fluffy, about 5 minutes. Blend
in vanilla, egg and sour cream. Gradually add flour mixture, beating until smooth after each addition. Stir in nuts and chocolate.
Drop by scant quarter cupfuls onto baking sheets, leaving 2 inches
between. Bake at 375° for 12 minutes or until lightly browned.
Remove carefully from sheets; cool on racks. Makes 2 dozen.

Chocolate Raisin Cookies: Prepare Chunky Chocolate Cookies as
directed, adding ½ cup raisins with the nuts.

Chattanooga Bars

1½ cups flour   ¾ teaspoon Calumet baking powder
¼ teaspoon salt   ½ cup chunky peanut butter
¼ cup butter or margarine, softened
¾ cup firmly packed brown sugar
3 tablespoons milk   1 teaspoon vanilla   1 egg
6 squares Baker's semi-sweet chocolate, melted

Mix flour, baking powder and salt. Cream peanut butter with butter; gradually beat in sugar. Add milk, vanilla and egg; blend well. Blend in flour mixture. Spread about two-thirds in greased and floured 13x9-inch pan. Drizzle most of the chocolate over dough. Pat remaining dough gently into pan; then drizzle with remaining chocolate. Bake at 375° for 18 to 20 minutes or until golden brown. Cool slightly in pan; then cut into bars or squares. Makes 2 dozen.

Fruit and Nut Bars

3 squares Baker's unsweetened chocolate
⅔ cup water   ½ cup granulated sugar
1 package (8 oz.) pitted dates, chopped
¼ cup butter or margarine   1 teaspoon vanilla
1¼ cups flour   ½ teaspoon salt
½ teaspoon baking soda   ¾ cup butter or margarine
¾ cup firmly packed light brown sugar
1¼ cups rolled oats   1 cup chopped nuts

Melt chocolate in water in saucepan over very low heat, stirring constantly. Add granulated sugar and stir until dissolved. Add dates. Cook and stir until mixture thickens, about 5 minutes. Remove from heat. Blend in ¼ cup butter and the vanilla. Cool.

Mix flour, salt and soda. Cream ¾ cup butter. Gradually beat in brown sugar and continue beating until light and fluffy. Add flour mixture, blending well. Add oats and nuts; mix until crumbly. Press half into greased 13x9-inch pan. Spread evenly with the chocolate-date mixture; top with remaining nut mixture. Bake at 350° for 35 minutes. Cool slightly in pan; then cut into bars or squares. Serve warm with ice cream, if desired. Makes about 30.

Chocolate-Striped Bars

2¼ cups flour   ¼ teaspoon salt
½ teaspoon Calumet baking powder
1½ tablespoons Maxwell House or Yuban instant coffee
¼ cup water   1 cup butter or margarine
1 cup firmly packed light brown sugar
1 teaspoon almond extract (optional)
4 squares Baker's semi-sweet chocolate, chopped
½ cup chopped nuts   Bittersweet Glaze (page 85)

Mix flour, salt and baking powder. Dissolve instant coffee in water. Cream butter; gradually beat in sugar. Blend in dissolved coffee and the extract. Gradually add flour mixture, blending well after each addition. Stir in chopped chocolate and nuts. Press into 15x10-inch jelly roll pan. Bake at 350° for 25 minutes. Drizzle glaze in stripes across top. Cool. Cut into bars. Makes about 3½ dozen.

Macaroons

2 squares Baker's unsweetened chocolate
2 tablespoons butter or margarine   ⅓ cup sugar
2 eggs, slightly beaten   ¼ teaspoon salt
1 teaspoon vanilla
2⅔ cups (about) Baker's Angel Flake coconut

Melt chocolate with butter in saucepan over very low heat, stirring constantly until smooth. Remove from heat. Blend in sugar, eggs, salt and vanilla; beat well. Stir in coconut. Drop from teaspoon onto greased baking sheets, leaving 1½ inches between. Bake at 325° for 15 minutes. Cool on racks. Makes about 3 dozen.

Pinwheels and Checkerboards

2 cups flour
1 teaspoon Calumet baking powder
½ teaspoon salt
⅔ cup butter or margarine
1 cup sugar
1 egg
1 teaspoon vanilla
2 squares Baker's unsweetened chocolate, melted

Mix flour, baking powder and salt. Cream butter. Gradually add
sugar and continue beating until light and fluffy. Add egg and
vanilla; beat well. Gradually add flour mixture, mixing well after
each addition. Divide dough in half; blend chocolate into one half.
Use prepared doughs to make Pinwheels or Checkerboards.

Pinwheels: Roll chocolate and vanilla doughs separately between
sheets of waxed paper into 12x8-inch rectangles. Remove top sheets
of paper and invert vanilla dough onto chocolate dough. Remove
remaining papers. Roll up as for jelly roll; then wrap in waxed
paper. Chill until firm, at least 3 hours (or freeze 1 hour). Cut into
¼-inch slices and place on baking sheets. Bake at 375° about 10
minutes, or until cookies just begin to brown around edges. Cool
on racks. Makes about 4½ dozen.

Checkerboards: Set out small amount of milk. Roll chocolate and
vanilla doughs separately on lightly floured board into 9x4½-inch
rectangles. Brush chocolate dough lightly with milk and top with
vanilla dough. Using a long sharp knife, cut lengthwise into 3
strips, 1½ inches wide. Stack strips, alternating colors and brushing
each layer with milk. Cut lengthwise again into 3 strips, ½ inch
wide. Invert middle section so that colors are alternated; brush sides
with milk. Press strips together lightly to form a rectangle. Wrap in
waxed paper. Chill overnight. Cut into ⅛-inch slices, using a very
sharp knife. Place on baking sheets. Bake at 375° for about 8 minutes, or just until white portions begin to brown. Cool on racks.
Makes about 5 dozen.

Glazed Chocolate Cookies

2¾ cups flour   2½ teaspoons Calumet baking powder
½ teaspoon salt   ½ cup butter or margarine
½ cup shortening
1⅔ cups sugar   2 eggs
3 teaspoons vanilla
2 squares Baker's unsweetened chocolate, melted and cooled
Bittersweet Glaze (page 85)

Mix flour, baking powder and salt. Cream butter with shortening.
Gradually beat in sugar and continue beating until light and fluffy.
Add eggs, one at a time, beating thoroughly after each. Stir in
vanilla and chocolate. Gradually add flour mixture, blending
thoroughly after each addition. Shape into balls, using 1½ tablespoons for each. Place 2 inches apart on greased baking sheets.
Using flat-bottom glass, buttered and dipped in granulated sugar,
press cookies to 3-inch diameters. Bake at 375° about 10 minutes.
Cool on racks. Top with glaze. Makes 3½ dozen.

Chocolate Drop Cookies

1⅔ cups flour   ¼ teaspoon baking soda
¼ teaspoon salt   ½ cup butter or margarine
1 cup sugar
1 teaspoon vanilla   1 egg
2 squares Baker's unsweetened chocolate, melted and cooled
⅓ cup sour milk or buttermilk   ¾ cup chopped walnuts

Mix flour, soda and salt. Cream butter. Gradually beat in sugar.
Add vanilla and egg; beat well. Blend in chocolate. Alternately add
flour mixture and sour milk, mixing thoroughly after each addition. Fold in walnuts. Drop from teaspoon onto baking sheets. Bake
at 350° for 10 to 12 minutes. Cool on racks. Makes 3½ dozen.

Double Chocolate Cookies

6 squares Baker's semi-sweet chocolate
2 squares Baker's unsweetened chocolate
6 tablespoons butter   2 eggs   2 teaspoons vanilla
¾ cup sugar   ⅓ cup flour   ¼ teaspoon salt
1 teaspoon Calumet baking powder
1 cup coarsely chopped nuts
4 squares Baker's semi-sweet chocolate, coarsely chopped

Melt 6 squares semi-sweet and the unsweetened chocolate with butter over very low heat, stirring constantly. Remove from heat. Beat eggs and vanilla thoroughly. Gradually add sugar; beat until thickened. Beat in warm chocolate. Mix flour, salt and baking powder; add to chocolate mixture and stir well. Stir in nuts and chopped chocolate. Drop by rounded teaspoonfuls onto lightly greased baking sheets. Bake at 325° about 12 minutes. Makes 2½ to 3 dozen.

Crackle-Top Cookies

1¾ cups flour   2 teaspoons Calumet baking powder
1 teaspoon cinnamon   ¾ teaspoon salt
½ cup vegetable shortening
1⅔ cups firmly packed brown sugar
2 eggs   1 teaspoon vanilla
2 squares Baker's unsweetened chocolate,
melted and cooled
⅓ cup milk   ⅔ cup chopped nuts   Confectioners sugar

Mix flour, baking powder, cinnamon and salt. Cream shortening. Gradually beat in brown sugar and continue beating until light and fluffy. Beat in eggs and vanilla; stir in chocolate. Alternately add flour mixture and milk, beating after each addition until smooth. Stir in nuts. Chill until firm, 2 to 3 hours. Shape into 1-inch balls, roll in confectioners sugar and set on greased baking sheets. Bake at 350° for 20 minutes. Cool on racks. Makes 5 dozen.

Lacy Chocolate Crisps

½ cup light corn syrup   ⅓ cup butter or margarine
1 package (4 oz.) Baker's German's sweet chocolate
½ cup firmly packed light brown sugar
1 cup flour   ⅔ cup Baker's Angel Flake coconut

Bring corn syrup to a boil. Add butter and chocolate. Cook and stir over low heat until smooth. Remove from heat; stir in sugar, flour and coconut. Drop from tablespoon onto lightly greased baking sheets, leaving 3 inches between. Bake at 300° for 15 minutes, or until wafers bubble vigorously and develop lacy holes. Cool on sheets 2 minutes; lift with spatula and finish cooling on racks. (If wafers harden on sheets, return briefly to oven.) If desired, roll warm wafers over wooden spoon handle; cool. Fill with tinted sweetened whipped cream. Makes 2½ dozen.

Florentines

½ cup flour   ¼ teaspoon baking soda
Dash of salt   ¼ cup butter or margarine
⅓ cup firmly packed brown sugar
2 tablespoons light corn syrup   1 egg, well beaten
½ cup Baker's Angel Flake coconut   ½ teaspoon vanilla
2 squares Baker's semi-sweet chocolate
1 tablespoon butter or margarine

Mix flour, soda and salt. Cream ¼ cup butter. Gradually add sugar and beat until light and fluffy. Add corn syrup and egg; blend well. Stir in flour mixture, coconut and vanilla. Drop by half teaspoonfuls onto greased baking sheets, leaving 2 inches between. Bake at 350° about 10 minutes. Cool on baking sheets 1 minute; remove quickly and finish cooling on racks. (If wafers harden on sheets, return briefly to oven.) Melt chocolate and 1 tablespoon butter in saucepan over very low heat, stirring constantly until smooth. Drizzle over wafers. Makes 4 dozen.

DESSERTS

Fruited Chocolate Trifle

⅔ cup sugar
2 tablespoons cornstarch
⅛ teaspoon salt
2 eggs, slightly beaten
3 cups milk, scalded
3 squares Baker's unsweetened chocolate
3 tablespoons almond liqueur*
12 ladyfingers, split
1 pint fresh strawberries, hulled and halved
1 can (16 oz.) apricot halves, drained

Or use ½ teaspoon almond extract.

Combine sugar, cornstarch and salt in bowl. Add eggs and mix well. Gradually pour in hot milk, stirring constantly. Return to saucepan. Cook and stir over very low heat until mixture is smooth and thickened. Remove from heat. Add chocolate and liqueur; stir until chocolate is melted. Cool slightly.

Arrange half of the ladyfingers, fruits and chocolate custard in layers in a serving dish; repeat layers with remaining ingredients. Chill at least 2 hours. Before serving, garnish with sweetened whipped cream, Chocolate Cut-Outs (page 89) and additional strawberries, if desired. Makes 8 to 10 servings.

La Belle Chocolatiere Loaf

12 ladyfingers, split   5 eggs, separated
1 package (8 squares) Baker's semi-sweet chocolate
¼ cup sugar   ¼ cup water
1½ teaspoons vanilla

Line bottom and sides of 8 x 4-inch loaf pan with waxed paper;
then line with ladyfingers. Set remaining ladyfingers aside. Thoroughly beat egg yolks in small bowl; set aside.

Melt chocolate in saucepan over very low heat, stirring constantly
until smooth. Blend in sugar, water and egg yolks. Cook and stir
until smooth. Remove from heat and stir in vanilla. Cool. Beat
egg whites until stiff peaks form. Fold in chocolate mixture.
Spoon into loaf pan; top with remaining ladyfingers. Chill at
least 4 hours. Before serving, invert onto serving platter and
remove waxed paper. Garnish with sweetened whipped cream, if
desired. Makes 8 servings.

Note: Use clean eggs with no cracks in shells.

Elegant Chocolate Mousse

3 squares Baker's unsweetened chocolate
¾ cup water   ¾ cup sugar
⅛ teaspoon salt   3 egg yolks, slightly beaten
1½ teaspoons vanilla   1¾ cups heavy cream*
3 tablespoons sugar*   ¾ teaspoon vanilla*

*Or use 3½ cups thawed Cool Whip whipped topping.

Melt chocolate in water in saucepan over very low heat, stirring
constantly until smooth. Stir in ¾ cup sugar and the salt. Bring to
a boil over medium heat, stirring constantly. Reduce heat and simmer 5 minutes, stirring constantly.

Blend a small amount of the hot mixture into egg yolks; stir into remaining hot mixture. Cook and stir 1 minute longer. Cool to room temperature; then add 1½ teaspoons vanilla. Whip the cream with 3 tablespoons sugar and ¾ teaspoon vanilla until soft peaks form. Gradually blend in chocolate mixture. Spoon into 9-inch square pan or 1½-quart freezer container. Freeze until firm, at least 6 hours. Makes 8 servings.

Strawberry Chocolate Mousse

2 squares Baker's semi-sweet chocolate   ¼ cup water
2 packages (3 oz. each) cream cheese, at room temperature
¼ cup milk   1 tablespoon sugar
1¾ cups heavy cream*   3 tablespoons sugar*
¾ teaspoon vanilla*
1 pint fresh strawberries, hulled and sliced

*Or use 3½ cups thawed Cool Whip whipped topping.

Melt chocolate in water in saucepan over very low heat, stirring constantly until smooth. Cool. Beat 1 package of the cream cheese until smooth. Add milk and 1 tablespoon sugar; blend well. Whip cream with 3 tablespoons sugar and the vanilla until soft peaks form. Measure 2 cups and fold into cheese mixture; then fold in half of the strawberries. Spoon into 1½-quart souffle dish or straight-sided serving dish. Chill.

Meanwhile, beat remaining package of cream cheese until fluffy. Gradually blend in chocolate; then fold into remaining whipped cream. Spoon over strawberry mixture. Chill about 3 hours. Dip dish in warm water for a few seconds and unmold onto serving plate. Garnish with remaining strawberries and additional sweetened whipped cream, if desired. Makes 6 to 8 servings.

Brownie Alaska

1½ cups strawberry ice cream
2 cups pistachio ice cream
3 cups vanilla ice cream
1 baked 8-inch Fudgy Brownies layer, cooled (page 39)
3 egg whites   ¼ teaspoon salt
¼ teaspoon cream of tartar   6 tablespoons sugar
Choco-Mallow Sauce (page 78)

Soften each flavor ice cream just before using. Press strawberry ice cream into 1½-quart mixing bowl; freeze until firm. Repeat with pistachio and vanilla ice creams. Unmold ice cream onto brownie layer; return to freezer while preparing meringue.

Beat egg whites with salt and cream of tartar until foamy throughout. Gradually add sugar, 1 tablespoon at a time, and continue beating until meringue forms stiff peaks. Place ice cream-topped brownie layer on brown paper-lined baking sheet. Spread meringue over entire surface, sealing bottom completely. Bake at 450° for 5 to 6 minutes, or until meringue is golden brown. Transfer to serving platter and serve at once with sauce. If dessert is made ahead, cover and store in freezer. Remove from freezer 20 minutes before serving (for ease in slicing). Makes 10 servings.

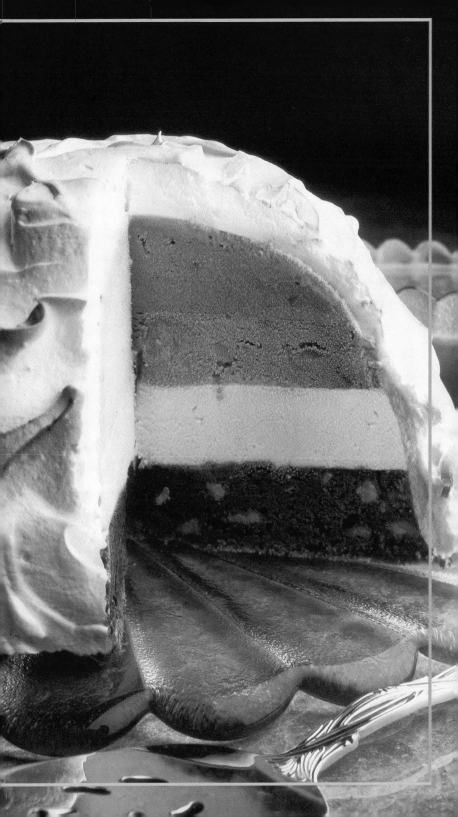

Souffle Supreme

2 squares Baker's unsweetened chocolate
1 cup milk
3 tablespoons butter or margarine
3 tablespoons flour
⅔ cup sugar
1 teaspoon vanilla
Dash of salt
6 egg whites
4 egg yolks
Chocolate Custard Sauce (page 79)

Melt chocolate in milk in saucepan over very low heat, stirring constantly until smooth. Remove from heat. Melt butter in saucepan; remove from heat and blend in flour. Gradually blend in chocolate mixture. Cook and stir over low heat until smooth and thickened. Stir in sugar, vanilla and salt. Cook and stir 3 to 4 minutes longer. Cool slightly.

Beat egg whites until stiff peaks form. Beat egg yolks until thick and light in color; blend in chocolate mixture. Fold in beaten egg whites. Pour into greased 1½-quart baking dish, individual souffle dishes or 1-quart souffle dish fitted with paper collar (see note). Place in pan containing 1 inch of hot water. Bake large souffle at 375° for 1 hour, individual souffles for 25 minutes. Serve at once with custard sauce. Makes 8 servings.

Note: To make paper collar, cut a piece of waxed paper long enough to wrap around dish and overlap slightly. Fold in half lengthwise; grease one side lightly with shortening. Wrap the doubled paper around dish, greased-side toward dish, extending it 2 inches above rim. Secure with string or tape. Remove paper collar before serving.

Chilled Chocolate-Rum Souffle

1 envelope unflavored gelatin
¼ cup cold water
4 squares Baker's unsweetened chocolate
¼ cup dark rum*
6 eggs, separated
⅔ cup sugar
¼ teaspoon salt
1 cup heavy cream**
2 tablespoons sugar**
½ teaspoon vanilla**

Or use ¼ cup milk and 1 teaspoon rum extract.
**Or use 2 cups thawed Cool Whip whipped topping.*

Soften gelatin in water. Melt chocolate in saucepan over very low heat, stirring constantly until smooth. Stir in rum and softened gelatin; stir until gelatin is dissolved. Remove from heat. Combine egg yolks and ⅔ cup sugar in top of double boiler. Place over hot water and beat with hand or electric mixer until thick and light in color. Remove from hot water. Blend in chocolate mixture; then pour into a bowl.

Beat egg whites with salt until stiff peaks form; fold into chocolate mixture. Whip cream with 2 tablespoons sugar and the vanilla until soft peaks form. Fold into chocolate mixture. Pour into buttered 1½-quart serving dish or 1-quart souffle dish fitted with paper collar. (For paper collar directions, see Souffle Supreme, at left.) Chill at least 3 hours. Garnish with additional sweetened whipped cream and chocolate curls, if desired. Makes 6 to 8 servings.

Note: Use clean eggs with no cracks in shells.

Pot de Creme au Chocolat

1 package (4 oz.) Baker's German's sweet chocolate
1¼ cups light cream or half and half   ¼ cup sugar
6 egg yolks, slightly beaten   1 teaspoon vanilla

Heat chocolate, cream and sugar in saucepan over very low heat, stirring constantly until chocolate is melted and mixture is smooth. Blend a small amount of the hot mixture into egg yolks; stir into remaining hot mixture. Cook and stir over medium heat until slightly thickened, about 5 minutes. Add vanilla and pour into pot de creme cups. Chill until set, about 3 hours. Garnish with chocolate curls, if desired. Makes 4 to 6 servings.

Chocolate Bavarian

3 eggs, separated   ⅓ cup sugar
1 envelope unflavored gelatin
¼ teaspoon salt   1½ cups milk
2 squares Baker's unsweetened chocolate
1 teaspoon vanilla   ⅓ cup sugar

Beat egg yolks in small bowl; set aside. Combine ⅓ cup sugar, the gelatin and salt in saucepan. Stir in milk; add chocolate. Cook and stir over low heat until chocolate is melted and mixture is smooth. Blend a small amount of hot mixture into egg yolks; stir into remaining hot mixture. Continue to cook and stir 3 minutes longer. Stir in vanilla and chill until slightly thickened.

Beat egg whites until foamy throughout. Gradually add ⅓ cup sugar and continue beating until mixture forms stiff peaks. Fold in chocolate mixture, blending well. Spoon into 4-cup mold or individual molds. Chill until firm, about 3 hours. Unmold. Garnish with sweetened whipped cream, if desired. Makes 8 servings.

Note: Use clean eggs with no cracks in shells.

Frozen Chocolate Bombe

1 purchased pound cake   ¼ cup almond liqueur*
1¾ cups heavy cream**   3 tablespoons sugar**
¾ teaspoon vanilla**
2 squares Baker's semi-sweet chocolate, melted and cooled
¼ cup chopped pecans
2 tablespoons finely chopped drained
maraschino cherries
3 squares Baker's semi-sweet chocolate
2 tablespoons butter or margarine

*Or use ¼ cup fruit nectar and ⅛ teaspoon almond extract.
**Or use 3½ cups thawed Cool Whip whipped topping.

Thinly slice pound cake; diagonally cut each piece in half. Line
1½-quart bowl with plastic wrap or strips of waxed paper; then line
with cake pieces, trimming as necessary to line bowl completely.
Sprinkle cake with liqueur. Set aside remaining cake pieces.

Whip the cream with sugar and vanilla until soft peaks form. Fold
melted chocolate into half of the whipped cream. Spoon into cake-
lined bowl. Fold pecans and cherries into remaining whipped
cream; spoon into bowl over chocolate mixture. Cover completely
with remaining cake pieces. Freeze until firm, about 4 hours.

Melt 3 squares chocolate with the butter in saucepan over very low
heat, stirring constantly until smooth. Cool slightly. Invert frozen
bombe onto serving plate. Remove plastic wrap. Spread chocolate
quickly and evenly over cake. Freeze about 10 minutes, or until
chocolate is firm. If frozen longer, remove from freezer 20 minutes
before serving (for ease in cutting). Makes 8 to 10 servings.

Almond Creme

2 packages (4 oz. each) Baker's German's
sweet chocolate
¼ cup water   ⅔ cup sweetened condensed milk
2 cups heavy cream   ½ teaspoon vanilla
½ cup toasted slivered blanched almonds

Melt chocolate in water in saucepan over very low heat, stirring
constantly until smooth. Cool. Combine chocolate, condensed
milk, cream and vanilla in large bowl of electric mixer. Chill; then
whip until soft peaks form. Fold in almonds. Spoon into 9-inch
square pan or 1½-quart freezer container. Freeze until firm, about
5 hours. Garnish with additional toasted almonds, if desired.
Makes 8 to 10 servings.

Chiffon au Chocolat

4 eggs, separated
6 squares Baker's semi-sweet chocolate
¼ cup cream or milk   1 teaspoon vanilla*
Dash of salt   ¼ cup sugar

*Or use 1 tablespoon brandy.

Beat egg yolks in small bowl; set aside. Melt chocolate in saucepan
over very low heat, stirring constantly until smooth. Remove from
heat. Blend in cream, vanilla and salt. Gradually add to egg
yolks; beat until thick and creamy. Beat egg whites until foamy
throughout. Gradually add sugar and continue beating until mixture forms stiff peaks. Fold in chocolate mixture. Spoon into individual dessert dishes or 1-quart serving bowl. Chill at least 2 hours.
Makes 8 servings.
Note: Use clean eggs with no cracks in shells.

CANDIES

Dorchester Fudge

1 package (8 squares) Baker's semi-sweet chocolate,
finely chopped
½ cup marshmallow topping
½ cup chopped nuts* (optional)
¼ cup butter or margarine, at room temperature
½ teaspoon vanilla   1½ cups sugar
⅔ cup evaporated milk

*Or use 1 cup Baker's Angel Flake coconut.

Place chocolate in a bowl with marshmallow topping, nuts, butter
and vanilla; set aside. Combine sugar and milk in 2-quart saucepan. Cook and stir over medium heat until mixture comes to a *full
rolling boil.* Keep at full rolling boil 5 minutes, stirring constantly.
Carefully pour boiling sugar syrup over chocolate mixture and stir
until chocolate is melted. Pour into buttered 8-inch square pan.
Chill until firm, about 1 hour. Cut into squares. Makes 1½ pounds
or about 3 dozen pieces.

Mocha Almond Fudge: Prepare Dorchester Fudge as directed,
using chopped toasted blanched almonds for the nuts and adding 2
teaspoons Maxwell House or Yuban instant coffee to milk mixture.

Peanut Butter Fudge: Prepare Dorchester Fudge as directed, substituting ½ cup peanut butter for the butter and nuts.

Fudge Shapes: Prepare Dorchester Fudge as directed, omitting the
nuts; cool slightly and pour fudge mixture onto waxed paper on
baking sheet. Top with waxed paper and roll with rolling pin until
½ inch thick. Remove top paper; run tines of fork across surface,
scoring fudge. Chill until firm; then cut into shapes with small
cookie cutters. Garnish with toasted almonds, if desired.

Pictured: Dorchester Fudge and Fudge Shapes, above.

Classic Fudge

2 squares Baker's unsweetened chocolate
¾ cup milk
2 cups sugar
Dash of salt
2 tablespoons butter or margarine
1 teaspoon vanilla

Place chocolate and milk in heavy saucepan. Stir constantly over very low heat until smooth and slightly thickened, about 5 minutes. Add sugar and salt; stir over medium heat until sugar is dissolved and mixture boils. Continue boiling, without stirring, until small amount of mixture forms a soft ball in cold water (or to a temperature of 234°).

Remove from heat; add butter and vanilla. *Do not stir.* Cool to lukewarm (110°). Beat until mixture begins to lose its gloss and holds its shape. Pour at once into buttered 8 x 4-inch loaf pan. Cool until set; then cut into squares. Let stand in pan until firm. Makes 1 pound or about 1½ dozen pieces.

Old-Fashioned Nut Bars

1 package (8 squares) Baker's semi-sweet chocolate*
⅔ cup raisins
⅔ cup chopped nuts

Or use 2 packages (4 oz. each) Baker's German's sweet chocolate.

Line bottom of 8 x 4-inch loaf pan with waxed paper, letting ends extend beyond pan. Melt chocolate in saucepan over very low heat, stirring constantly until smooth. Remove from heat and stir in raisins and nuts. Pour into loaf pan, spreading evenly. Tap pan several times to settle chocolate. Top with additional chopped or halved nuts, if desired. Chill until chocolate is firm. Lift from pan;

remove waxed paper and cut into bars or squares. Makes 16 to 24.

Raisin Nut Cups: Spoon melted chocolate mixture into 3 dozen paper or aluminum foil bonbon cups.

Coconut Apricot Bars: Prepare Old-Fashioned Nut Bars as directed, substituting ½ cup chopped dried apricots and ½ cup Baker's Angel Flake coconut for the raisins and nuts.

Tutti Frutti Bars: Prepare Old-Fashioned Nut Bars as directed, substituting ⅓ cup *each* finely cut candied pineapple, cherries, citron and toasted slivered blanched almonds for the raisins and nuts.

Nut Clusters

1 package (8 squares) Baker's semi-sweet chocolate
1½ to 2 cups whole or halved nuts*

Or use 1⅓ cups (about) toasted Baker's Angel Flake coconut.

Melt chocolate in saucepan over very low heat, stirring constantly until smooth. Remove from heat. Add nuts; mix lightly to coat completely. Drop mixture from teaspoon onto waxed paper on baking sheet. Chill until firm. Makes about 2 dozen.

Chewy Chocolate Candies

½ pound soft caramels
2 tablespoons heavy cream
1 cup (about) pecan halves
4 squares Baker's semi-sweet chocolate, melted and cooled

Heat caramels with cream in saucepan over very low heat, stirring constantly. Cool 10 minutes. Set pecans on lightly buttered baking sheets in clusters of 3. Spoon caramel mixture over nuts, leaving outer ends of nuts showing. Let stand to set, about 30 minutes. Spread melted chocolate over caramel mixture. Makes 2 dozen.

Truffles

5 tablespoons unsalted butter
1 egg yolk
⅔ cup sifted confectioners sugar
3 squares Baker's semi-sweet chocolate,
melted and cooled
1 teaspoon vanilla
½ cup finely chopped nuts or toasted
Baker's Angel Flake coconut

Cream butter with egg yolk; gradually add sugar, blending well. Stir in chocolate and vanilla. Chill until firm enough to handle. Shape into 1-inch balls. Roll in nuts. Chill until set. Store in refrigerator. Makes about 30.

Note: Use clean egg with no cracks in shells.

Orange Truffle Cups: Prepare Truffles as directed, adding 1 to 2 tablespoons orange liqueur and ¼ teaspoon grated orange rind with the vanilla and omitting nuts. Spoon or pipe mixture into Bonbon Chocolate Crinkle Cups (page 91). Chill.

Chocolate-Coated Almond Truffles: Prepare Truffles as directed, adding 2 tablespoons finely ground almonds and ¼ teaspoon almond extract with the vanilla and using ¼ cup ground almonds for the nuts. Shape truffle mixture into balls; dip bottoms into ground almonds. Place on rack and chill. Partially melt 5 squares Baker's semi-sweet chocolate in saucepan over very low heat, stirring constantly. Remove from heat and stir until completely melted. Spoon over truffles to cover tops and sides. Drizzle any remaining chocolate from a fork to make design over tops. Chill.

Pictured: Truffles, Orange Truffle Cups and Chocolate-Coated Almond Truffles, above.

Coconut Delights

2⅔ cups (about) Baker's Angel Flake coconut
1½ cups confectioners sugar
¼ cup butter or margarine, at room temperature
2 tablespoons hot water
1 teaspoon vanilla
1 package (8 squares) Baker's semi-sweet chocolate*

Or use 2 packages (4 oz. each) Baker's German's sweet chocolate.

Combine coconut, sugar, butter, water and vanilla in large bowl; stir until thoroughly blended. Using rounded teaspoonful of mixture for each, shape into ovals. Place on waxed paper and set aside.

Partially melt chocolate in saucepan over very low heat, stirring constantly. Remove from heat and stir until entirely melted. Holding each candy on a fork, spoon chocolate over to completely cover, allowing excess to drip back into pan. Place on waxed paper and let stand until chocolate is firm. Makes about 2 dozen.

Almond Coconut Delights: Toast about 30 whole blanched almonds. Prepare Coconut Delights as directed; press about 1 teaspoon coconut mixture around each almond and shape into balls. Cover with chocolate as directed. Makes 2½ dozen.

French Chocolates

1 package (8 squares) Baker's unsweetened chocolate
1 package (4 oz.) Baker's German's sweet chocolate
1 can (15 oz.) sweetened condensed milk
1 cup (about) finely chopped nuts

Melt chocolates together in saucepan over very low heat, stirring constantly until smooth. Add condensed milk and mix until smooth and well blended. Cool a few minutes. Shape into balls, using about 1 teaspoon for each. Roll in nuts. Makes about 6 dozen.

Bonbon Cups

1 package (8 squares) Baker's semi-sweet chocolate
1 cup sifted confectioners sugar
1 tablespoon milk
1 tablespoon light corn syrup
½ cup chopped mixed candied fruits
1 teaspoon rum extract (optional)
2 tablespoons butter or margarine

Melt 4 squares of the chocolate in saucepan over very low heat, stirring constantly until smooth. Remove from heat. Add sugar, milk and corn syrup. Stir in fruits and extract. Spoon into 3 dozen paper or aluminum foil bonbon cups; chill.

Melt remaining 4 squares chocolate with the butter in saucepan over very low heat, stirring constantly until smooth. Cool slightly; spoon onto fruit filling in cups, mounding the chocolate. Chill until firm. Store in refrigerator. Makes 3 dozen.

Chocolate Creams

1 package (8 squares) Baker's semi-sweet chocolate
½ cup butter or margarine
1¾ cups sifted confectioners sugar
2 tablespoons light cream or half and half
1 teaspoon vanilla
1 cup finely chopped nuts or grated Baker's semi-sweet chocolate

Melt chocolate with butter in saucepan over very low heat, stirring constantly until smooth. Blend in sugar, cream and vanilla. Chill about 30 minutes. Shape into ½-inch balls and roll in nuts. Store in refrigerator. Makes about 4½ dozen.

Decorator Chocolates

2 packages (16 squares) Baker's semi-sweet
chocolate, finely grated or chopped
Decorator Frosting

Place chocolate in top of 1½-quart double boiler. Pour boiling
water into bottom of double boiler and place top over water. Stir
constantly and rapidly until chocolate is melted. (Do not place pan
over direct heat.) Fasten candy thermometer inside double boiler
with bulb immersed in chocolate. Stir rapidly in circular motion
until temperature reaches 130°. Remove top of double boiler.

Discard hot water and refill bottom pan with cold tap water.
Replace top and stir chocolate rapidly, scraping sides often, until
chocolate cools to 83°. Remove top of double boiler; place thermometer in bottom pan and add hot water to bring temperature to
85°. Replace top pan. Spoon chocolate into about 3 dozen small
candy molds. Tap molds on counter to eliminate air bubbles. Chill
until firm. Unmold. Using plastic-lined decorating bags or parchment paper cones fitted with fine (small opening) decorating tips,
pipe Decorator Frosting onto candies. Makes about 3 dozen.

Note: Work in a draft-free, cool (60° to 70°), dry room.

Decorator Frosting: Cream ¼ cup butter or margarine in bowl;
add 1 teaspoon vanilla. Alternately add 2 cups sifted confectioners
sugar with about 2 tablespoons milk until of decorating consistency, beating after each addition until smooth. Measure
¼ cup and blend in ½ square melted Baker's semi-sweet chocolate.
Tint remaining frosting one or more colors with food coloring.

*Pictured: Almond Toffee, page 72, and Nut Crunch, page 73; Decorator
Chocolates, above.*

Almond Toffee

1 cup butter or margarine
1 cup sugar
3 tablespoons water
1 tablespoon light corn syrup
⅓ cup chopped toasted blanched almonds
1 package (8 squares) Baker's semi-sweet chocolate
⅔ cup chopped toasted blanched almonds

Melt butter in heavy 2-quart saucepan over very low heat. Add
sugar and stir until mixture starts to boil. Combine water and corn
syrup; blend into sugar mixture. Cook and stir over medium heat
until mixture comes to a boil. Reduce heat; cover and cook 3 minutes. Uncover and cook gently, stirring frequently to prevent burning, until a small amount of mixture forms a hard and brittle
thread in cold water (or to a temperature of 300°). Remove from
heat. Stir in ⅓ cup almonds. Spread evenly in well-buttered 15 x 10-
inch jelly roll pan. Let stand until almost cool to the touch.
Melt 4 squares of the chocolate in saucepan over very low heat, stirring constantly until smooth. Spread over toffee; then sprinkle
with ⅓ cup of the remaining almonds. Let stand until chocolate is
firm. Turn toffee out onto waxed paper. (Toffee may break.) Melt
remaining 4 squares chocolate and spread over toffee. Sprinkle with
remaining ⅓ cup almonds. Let stand until chocolate is firm. Break
into pieces. Makes about 1½ pounds.

Chocolate Brittle Drops

4 squares Baker's semi-sweet chocolate
1½ cups (½ lb.) coarsely crushed peanut brittle

Melt chocolate in saucepan over very low heat, stirring constantly.
Remove from heat and stir in peanut brittle. Drop from teaspoon
onto waxed paper. Let stand until chocolate is firm. Makes 2 dozen.

Nut Crunch

½ cup chopped nuts
½ cup butter or margarine
¾ cup firmly packed brown sugar
6 squares Baker's semi-sweet chocolate,
coarsely chopped

Sprinkle nuts into lightly buttered 8-inch square pan. Melt butter in heavy saucepan over very low heat. Add sugar and bring to a full rolling boil over medium heat, stirring constantly. Reduce heat and boil gently 4 minutes, stirring occasionally. Pour evenly over nuts in pan; sprinkle with chocolate. Cover with aluminum foil for 2 minutes to soften chocolate; then spread evenly. Chill until firm. Remove from pan; cut or break into pieces. Makes about 1 pound.

White-Capped Bars

½ cup chopped pecans
1 tablespoon butter or margarine
1⅓ cups miniature marshmallows
1 package (8 squares) Baker's semi-sweet chocolate, melted

Saute pecans in butter in small skillet over low heat for 3 to 5 minutes, stirring constantly. Set aside to cool. Line bottom of 8 x 4-inch loaf pan with waxed paper, letting paper extend beyond pan. Arrange half of the marshmallows in pan; fill spaces between with pecans. Pour chocolate evenly over marshmallow-nut mixture, using fork to distribute chocolate. Tap pan several times to settle chocolate. Press remaining marshmallows lightly into top. Let stand until chocolate is firm. Lift out candy, remove paper and cut into bars. Makes about 2 dozen.

Chocolate-Dipped Morsels

4 squares Baker's semi-sweet chocolate
Assorted morsel centers

Melt chocolate in saucepan over very low heat, stirring constantly until smooth. Insert wooden picks or skewers into fruit and marshmallow centers. Dip quickly, one at a time, into chocolate. (To dip pretzels or nuts, stir into chocolate; then remove with fork.) Let stand or chill on rack or waxed paper until chocolate is firm. For best eating quality, chill dipped fresh or canned fruits and serve the same day. Makes 1 to 1½ dozen.

Suggested Morsel Centers

Fruits: Firm strawberries, ½-inch banana slices, fresh pineapple wedges or drained canned pineapple chunks, peeled orange slices, orange wedges, well-drained stemmed maraschino cherries, dried figs, dried dates or dried apricots.

Unsalted Pretzels and Large Marshmallows

Nuts: Walnut or pecan halves or whole almonds or Brazil nuts.

TOPPINGS

Crackle Sundae Sauce

2 tablespoons butter or margarine
½ cup finely chopped pecans
4 squares Baker's semi-sweet chocolate*

Or use 1 package (4 oz.) Baker's German's sweet chocolate.

Melt butter in small heavy skillet over low heat. Add pecans and saute, stirring constantly, until pecans are light golden brown. Remove from heat. Add chocolate and stir until melted and smooth. Serve warm over ice cream. Store any leftover sauce in refrigerator. Reheat over hot water before serving. Makes ¾ cup.

Framingham Fudge Sauce

5 squares Baker's unsweetened chocolate
1 cup heavy cream*   1½ cups sugar
¼ teaspoon salt   ¼ cup light corn syrup
2 tablespoons butter or margarine
½ teaspoon cinnamon (optional)

Or use ¾ cup milk.

Melt chocolate in cream in saucepan over very low heat, stirring constantly until smooth. Add sugar, salt and corn syrup. Cook and stir until sugar is completely dissolved. Remove from heat. Stir in butter and cinnamon. Serve warm over cake, pudding, ice cream, custard or fruit. Store any leftover sauce in refrigerator and reheat over hot water before serving. Makes 2½ cups.

Pictured: Crackle Sundae Sauce, above; Bittersweet Sauce, page 79; Framingham Fudge Sauce, above.

Regal Chocolate Sauce

2 squares Baker's unsweetened chocolate
6 tablespoons water
½ cup sugar
Dash of salt
3 tablespoons butter or margarine
¼ teaspoon vanilla

Melt chocolate in water in saucepan over very low heat, stirring constantly until smooth. Add sugar and salt. Cook and stir about 5 minutes, or until sugar is dissolved and mixture is very slightly thickened. Remove from heat. Blend in butter and vanilla. Serve warm over ice cream or fruit. Store any leftover sauce in refrigerator and reheat over hot water before serving. Makes 1 cup.

Minted Chocolate Sauce: Prepare Regal Chocolate Sauce as directed, adding ⅓ cup crushed white peppermint candies (or ¼ teaspoon peppermint extract) with the butter and vanilla.

Choco-Mallow Sauce

1 package (4 oz.) Baker's German's sweet chocolate
1⅓ cups evaporated milk
1 cup miniature marshmallows

Place all ingredients in saucepan. Stir constantly over very low heat until mixture is smooth. Serve warm or cool over cake, pudding or frozen desserts. Store any leftover sauce in refrigerator. Reheat over hot water, if desired. Makes 2 cups.

Chocolate Custard Sauce

1 egg, slightly beaten
¼ cup sugar
¼ teaspoon salt
1½ cups milk
1 square Baker's unsweetened chocolate, melted
½ teaspoon vanilla

Combine egg, sugar, salt and milk in saucepan. Cook and stir over medium heat until mixture begins to thicken slightly and coats a metal spoon, about 5 minutes. Remove from heat. Stir in chocolate and vanilla. Beat with hand or electric mixer until blended. Cover surface with plastic wrap. Chill. Serve over fruit, desserts or cake. Store any leftover sauce in refrigerator. Makes 1½ cups.

Bittersweet Sauce

2 squares Baker's unsweetened chocolate, chopped
½ cup sugar
½ cup hot milk
Dash of salt
¾ teaspoon vanilla

Place all ingredients in blender container. Cover and blend at high speed until smooth, about 1 minute, turning blender off and scraping down sides after 30 seconds. Serve over pudding, cake or ice cream. Store any leftover sauce in refrigerator. Makes 1 cup.

Bittersweet Mocha Sauce: Prepare Bittersweet Sauce as directed, substituting 1 tablespoon Maxwell House or Yuban instant coffee dissolved in ¼ cup hot water for the milk. Blend in ¼ cup light cream before serving.

Hungarian Chocolate Frosting

5 squares Baker's unsweetened chocolate
3 cups confectioners sugar
⅓ cup hot water   2 egg yolks*
8 tablespoons (1 stick) butter or margarine,
at room temperature

Or use 1 whole egg.

Melt chocolate in saucepan over very low heat, stirring constantly until smooth. Pour into mixer bowl. Add sugar and water, all at once; blend well. Add egg yolks, one at a time, beating well after each addition. Add butter, 1 tablespoon at a time, beating thoroughly after each addition. (If frosting is too soft to spread, place bowl in larger bowl of cold water and stir until of spreading consistency.) Makes about 2⅔ cups, or enough to cover tops and sides of two 8- or 9-inch layers or the top and sides of one 13 x 9-inch cake or 10-inch tube cake.

Note: Use clean eggs with no cracks in shells.

Chocolate Butter Frosting

6 tablespoons butter or margarine   Dash of salt
1 pound (4 cups) confectioners sugar
2 squares Baker's unsweetened chocolate,
melted and cooled
4 tablespoons (about) milk   1½ teaspoons vanilla

Cream butter with salt. Gradually beat in part of the sugar. Blend in chocolate. Alternately add remaining sugar with milk until of spreading consistency, beating after each addition until smooth. Blend in vanilla. Makes 3 cups, or enough to cover tops and sides of two 8- or 9-inch layers or the top and sides of one 13 x 9-inch cake.

Mocha Frosting

2 tablespoons Maxwell House or Yuban instant coffee
1½ teaspoons warm water   1 teaspoon vanilla
¾ cup butter or margarine, at room temperature
2 cups confectioners sugar
3 squares Baker's unsweetened chocolate,
melted and cooled
2 eggs

Dissolve instant coffee in water; then add vanilla. Cream butter.
Gradually beat in sugar and continue beating until light and fluffy.
Blend in chocolate and coffee. Add eggs, one at a time, beating
until light and fluffy after each. Makes 3½ cups, or enough
to cover tops and sides of three 8- or 10 x 5-inch layers or two
9-inch layers.
Note: Use clean eggs with no cracks in shells.

Classic Fudge Frosting

4 squares Baker's unsweetened chocolate
2 tablespoons butter or margarine
1 pound (4 cups) confectioners sugar
Dash of salt   ½ cup milk
1 teaspoon vanilla

Melt chocolate with butter over very low heat, stirring constantly
until smooth. Remove from heat. Combine sugar, salt, milk and
vanilla. Add chocolate, blending well. If necessary, let stand until of
spreading consistency, stirring occasionally. Spread quickly, adding
a small amount of additional milk if frosting thickens. Makes
about 2½ cups, or enough to cover tops and sides of two 8- or 9-
inch layers, the top and sides of one 9-inch square or 13 x 9-inch
cake, or the tops of 24 cupcakes.

Chocolate Fondue

1 package (8 squares) Baker's semi-sweet chocolate
⅔ cup milk
¼ cup sugar
Dash of cinnamon
Assorted accompaniments

Place chocolate, milk, sugar and cinnamon in saucepan. Stir constantly over very low heat until smooth. Pour into fondue pot or small chafing dish and keep warm while serving. (If heated longer than ½ hour, thin with additional milk to maintain dipping consistency.) Or, pour into demitasse cups or small glasses and serve immediately. Accompany fondue with fruit or cake (see below), spearing each with long-handled fork and swirling through chocolate one piece at a time. Makes about 4 servings.

Brandied Chocolate Fondue: Prepare Chocolate Fondue as directed, substituting 6 tablespoons light cream or half and half for the milk, omitting the cinnamon and adding 3 tablespoons brandy.

Double Chocolate Fondue: Prepare Chocolate Fondue as directed, adding 1 package (4 oz.) Baker's German's sweet chocolate and increasing milk to ¾ cup. Makes about 8 servings.

Honey Peanut Fondue: Prepare Chocolate Fondue as directed, omitting sugar, reducing milk to ½ cup and adding ½ cup honey and ¼ cup creamy peanut butter. Makes about 6 servings.

Suggested Accompaniments

Fruits: Fresh fruits, such as seedless red or green grapes, strawberries, apple slices, banana or pineapple chunks, pear wedges, peeled orange or kiwi slices or stemmed cherries; dried fruits, such as apricots, figs or prunes.

Cakes: Strips of fruitcake or toasted pound cake.

Note: Recipe may be doubled.

Continental Flair Frosting

1 cup sugar
1 cup heavy cream or evaporated milk
4 squares Baker's unsweetened chocolate
½ cup butter or margarine, at room temperature
1 teaspoon rum extract or vanilla

Combine sugar and cream in saucepan. Bring to a boil over
medium heat, stirring constantly. Reduce heat and simmer gently
for 6 minutes. Remove from heat. Add chocolate and stir until
chocolate is melted. Blend in butter and rum extract. Chill until
mixture begins to thicken; then beat until thick, creamy and of
spreading consistency. Makes about 2½ cups, or enough to cover
tops and sides of two 8- or 9-inch cake layers, the top and sides of
one 9-inch square or 13 x 9-inch cake, or the tops of 24 cupcakes.

Cream Cheese Frosting

4 squares Baker's semi-sweet chocolate
1 package (3 oz.) cream cheese, at room temperature
1 tablespoon light cream or milk
¼ teaspoon salt   1 cup sifted confectioners sugar
½ teaspoon vanilla

Melt chocolate in saucepan over very low heat, stirring constantly
until smooth. Remove from heat. Blend in cream cheese, cream
and salt. Gradually beat in sugar and continue beating until
smooth. Add vanilla. Makes 1 cup, or enough to cover tops of two
8-inch layers, the top of one 9-inch square cake or the tops of
1 dozen cupcakes.

Chocolate Glaze

3 squares Baker's semi-sweet chocolate*
3 tablespoons water
1 tablespoon butter or margarine
1 cup sifted confectioners sugar
Dash of salt
½ teaspoon vanilla

Or use 1 package (4 oz.) Baker's German's sweet chocolate.

Place chocolate, water and butter in saucepan. Stir constantly over very low heat until mixture is smooth. Remove from heat. Combine sugar and salt in bowl. Gradually blend in chocolate mixture and vanilla. For thinner glaze, add a small amount of hot water. For thicker glaze, cool until of desired consistency. Makes about ¾ cup, or enough for a 9- or 10-inch tube cake, 8- or 9-inch layer cake, 13 x 9-inch cake or a 10-inch cake roll.

Bittersweet Glaze

2 squares Baker's unsweetened chocolate
2 tablespoons butter or margarine
Dash of salt
1¾ cups confectioners sugar
3 tablespoons (about) hot water

Melt chocolate with butter in saucepan over very low heat, stirring constantly until smooth. Remove from heat and add salt. Alternately add sugar with water until of spreading consistency. Makes 1 cup, or enough for a 9- or 10-inch tube cake, 9-inch square cake, 10-inch cake roll or about 3½ dozen cookies.

CHOCOLATE
KNOW-HOW

Chocolate Decorations

Special touches such as these make any dessert more delightful. Chocolate curls, trees, butterflies, leaves, cut-outs and doodles are easy to make, just follow the directions below.

Curls

Place 1 or more squares Baker's semi-sweet or unsweetened chocolate or several 3-square strips of Baker's German's sweet chocolate on a piece of aluminum foil. Let stand in warm place (90° to 100°) or in gas oven with burning pilot light until very slightly softened, 5 to 10 minutes. (Wrapped chocolate may also be warmed by holding between hands.)

Shave chocolate from bottom into curls, using long strokes of vegetable peeler or small sharp knife. Quick strokes make tight curls; slow strokes make looser curls.

If you prefer, melt 4 squares Baker's semi-sweet or unsweetened chocolate or 1 package (4 oz.) Baker's German's sweet chocolate in saucepan over very low heat, stirring constantly. Spread chocolate with spatula or flat pastry brush in a very thin layer on underside of baking sheet. Chill until firm but still pliable, about 10 minutes.

To make curls, slip tip of straight-side metal spatula under chocolate. Push spatula firmly along baking sheet, under chocolate, until a curl forms. Width of curls will vary depending on the width of spatula. If chocolate is too firm to curl, let stand a few minutes at room temperature; chill again if it becomes too soft.

Carefully pick up each chocolate curl by inserting a wooden pick in center. Lift onto waxed paper-lined baking sheet. Chill until firm, about 15 minutes. Arrange on pies, desserts and cakes.

Trees and Butterflies

Melt 2 squares Baker's semi-sweet chocolate or ½ package Baker's German's sweet chocolate in saucepan over very low heat, stirring constantly. Remove from heat and stir occasionally until cool to the touch (about 83°).

Meanwhile, cut 6x4-inch aluminum foil or parchment rectangles. You will need 2 rectangles for *each* tree (total of 12); one rectangle for each butterfly (total of 6). Fold each rectangle in half with narrow ends together. Open flat, leaving crease down center. Using the dull tip of a spoon handle or the wooden end of a kitchen match, draw the following marks on the foil:

For trees, make a 3-inch line on each center crease, representing a tree trunk. Draw 4 overlapping and diminishing-size triangles on each trunk to form tree branches. (Triangles should be flush with trunk at both ends.)
Pour chocolate into plastic-lined decorating bag fitted with fine writing tip. Pipe chocolate over each tree outline, overlapping branches and trunk lines where they intersect. (Lines of piped chocolate should be about ¼ inch thick.) Reserve leftover chocolate.

For butterflies, make an oval 1½ inches long and ½ inch wide around each center crease, representing a butterfly body. Draw antennae; outline wings so they extend about 1 inch on either side of body. Draw matching lacy lines in wings for design.
Pour chocolate into plastic-lined decorating bag fitted with fine writing tip. Pipe chocolate over outlines, overlapping wing patterns and outlines where they meet and where they join the body. (Lines of piped chocolate should be about ⅛ inch thick.) Fill in oval bodies completely, using all remaining chocolate.

Lift foil rectangles into 13x9- and/or 9x9-inch pans so half of each rectangle rests on the pan bottom and the other half is propped up against pan side. (Tree branches will be at right angles to the trunk; butterfly wings will be at right angles to each other.) Chill until chocolate is firm, at least 30 minutes.

Work quickly, and carefully separate foil from chocolate designs with a spatula.

For trees, drizzle some of the reserved chocolate over 2 trunks; gently press together to join. Repeat with remaining chocolate and tree trunks. Chill until firm, at least 30 minutes.

Use trees and butterflies to decorate frosted cakes, cream pies, puddings and other desserts. Makes 6.

Leaves

Melt 4 squares Baker's semi-sweet or unsweetened chocolate or 1 package (4 oz.) Baker's German's sweet chocolate in saucepan over very low heat, stirring constantly. Spread chocolate with flat brush or narrow spatula over *undersides* of washed and dried ivy, dogwood, lemon, holly or philodendron leaves, forming a smooth thick coating. Place on waxed paper-lined baking sheet and chill until chocolate is firm, about 15 minutes. Carefully peel away leaves from chocolate. Set chocolate leaves on desserts and frosted cakes. Makes 15 to 20.

For serving-size chocolate leaves, spread melted chocolate on 1 large, 2 medium or 4 small cabbage leaves. Fill prepared leaves with mousse, ice cream or fresh fruit pieces.

Cut-Outs

Melt 4 squares Baker's semi-sweet chocolate or 1 package (4 oz.) Baker's German's sweet chocolate in saucepan over very low heat, stirring constantly. Pour onto waxed paper-lined baking sheet; spread to ⅛-inch thickness with spatula. Chill until firm, about 15 minutes. Cut into desired shapes with cookie cutters or sharp knife and *at once* lift gently from paper with spatula. Set on desserts and frosted cakes. Makes about 20 (1 inch) shapes.

Doodles

Melt 1 square Baker's semi-sweet chocolate or two 3-square strips Baker's German's sweet chocolate with 1½ teaspoons butter or margarine in saucepan over very low heat, stirring constantly. Blend in 1½ tablespoons milk. Pour from tip of teaspoon, making lacy circles and free-form designs directly on surface of set pudding, ice cream, chiffon pie or frosted cake. Chill until chocolate is firm, about 15 minutes. Makes 6 to 8 doodles, each about 2 inches in diameter.

Drizzle

Melt 2 squares Baker's semi-sweet or unsweetened chocolate with 2 teaspoons butter or margarine in saucepan over very low heat, stirring constantly. (Or use 1 package [4 oz.] Baker's German's sweet chocolate and 3 tablespoons water.) Drizzle from tip of teaspoon over candies or cookies or around top edge of frosted cake, letting chocolate run down sides. Keep in cool place until chocolate is firm, about 30 minutes. Makes about ¼ cup.

Grated Chocolate

Chill 1 or more squares Baker's semi-sweet or unsweetened chocolate or several 3-square strips of Baker's German's sweet chocolate and a hand grater; then grate chocolate quickly to prevent melting. Sprinkle grated chocolate over pudding and ice cream; fold into sweetened whipped cream or thawed Cool Whip whipped topping; or sprinkle over lace paper doily on a frosted layer cake (later removing doily carefully).

Chocolate Containers

An elegant way to serve the best berries of the season, a special dessert or a cream confection .

Crinkle Cups

Melt 6 squares Baker's semi-sweet chocolate or 1 package (4 oz.) Baker's German's sweet chocolate with 2 tablespoons butter or margarine in saucepan over very low heat, stirring constantly. Spread chocolate over inside of 10 aluminum foil baking cups, using a spoon to completely push chocolate over all surfaces in a thin layer. Set cups in muffin pans. Chill until firm, about 1 hour. Fill with chiffon, pudding, ice cream or berries. Remove foil cups. Makes 6 using sweet chocolate or 10 using semi-sweet chocolate.

For Bonbon Chocolate Crinkle Cups, spread chocolate in 30 paper or aluminum foil bonbon cups. Fill with candy mixtures, liqueurs or small berries.

How to Melt Chocolate

No matter what method is chosen, chocolate should always be melted with gentle heat because it scorches easily. If chocolate is to be melted alone, make certain that the container and stirring utensil used are absolutely dry. A tiny drop of moisture will cause the chocolate to become lumpy and stiff. If this happens, the chocolate can be brought back to a smooth consistency by stirring in one teaspoon of vegetable shortening for each ounce of chocolate. Remember that unsweetened chocolate liquifies when melted, but semi-sweet and sweet cooking chocolate tend to hold their shapes until stirred. Chop chocolate coarsely for faster melting, if desired.

Over Very Low Heat: Place unwrapped chocolate in a small saucepan over very low heat. Stir constantly until chocolate is melted and smooth. Remove from heat.

Over Hot Water: Place unwrapped chocolate in top of double boiler. Melt over hot (not boiling) water, stirring constantly until smooth, 10 to 12 minutes. Or use a custard cup or saucepan set in a pan of water.

In Liquid: In some recipes, the chocolate may be melted with the shortening or liquid over very low direct heat, stirring constantly. If necessary, continue stirring until thoroughly blended and smooth.

In Oven: Place squares of chocolate, unwrapped or wrapped with folded tabs up, on a pan or piece of foil. Place in an oven with low heat just until chocolate melts.

In a Microwave Oven: Place one square of chocolate, unwrapped or wrapped with folded tabs up, in a glass or china dish or pie plate. Heat in microwave oven until melted, 1 to 2 minutes. (Time may vary by brand and model of oven.) Add 10 seconds for each additional square of chocolate being melted.

Candy-Dipping and Glazing: To keep the chocolate glossy, always place it over hot water and heat only until partially melted; then remove from water and stir until chocolate is entirely melted.

BAKER'S Chocolate Products

Unsweetened Chocolate is made from a blend of fine cocoa beans—roasted, crushed and ground between great heated rollers into a ruddy-brown liquor, satin-smooth and rich in cocoa butter. Nothing is added or removed from this fragrant chocolate liquor. This fine chocolate is molded and wrapped in 1-ounce squares, each grooved to break easily into ½-ounce pieces. The chocolate is sold in 8-ounce packages.

Semi-Sweet Chocolate is a superb blend of ingredients, with just enough sugar, extra cocoa butter and flavorings added to give it the satiny gloss so desired in candies. This chocolate is also made in 1-ounce squares and sold in 8-ounce packages.

German's Sweet Chocolate was created by Samuel German in 1852 as a quality snack-type chocolate bar. It's a special blend of chocolate, enriched with cocoa butter and sugar. This unique formula is the basis of a chocolate that retains its rich, full-bodied flavor in recipes. The chocolate is sold in 4-ounce packages.

How to Store Chocolate

Store chocolate in a dry, cool place, below 75° if possible. At higher temperatures the cocoa butter melts and rises to the surface. When this occurs, chocolate develops a pale gray color known as "bloom." This condition does not impair flavor or quality and the original color will return when the chocolate is melted.

To prevent chocolate from developing bloom during hot humid weather, refrigerate in the original wrappings. Remove from the refrigerator as needed, since bloom may develop as the chocolate comes to room temperature.

Chocolate Substitutions

Most recipes are so carefully developed and tested that you are more sure of success when you follow the recipe exactly. Generally, it is best not to substitute a sweet chocolate for an unsweetened chocolate and vice versa.

INDEX

94

Chiffon, 28
Chocolate Mousse au Rhum, 24
Classic Meringue, 31
Coconut Chocolate, 27
Crumb Crust, 35
Fudge Brownie, 26
German Chocolate, 34
Peppermint, 27
Pie Shell, 35
Southern Chocolate Pecan, 32
Sweet Coconut, 26
Pie Shell, 35
Pinwheels and Checkerboards, 44
Pot de Creme au Chocolat, 58
Raisin Nut Cups, 65
Regal Chocolate Sauce, 78
Ricotta Cheesecake, 20
Sauces
Bittersweet, 79
Bittersweet Mocha, 79
Chocolate Custard, 79
Choco-Mallow, 78
Crackle Sundae, 76

Framingham Fudge, 76
Minted Chocolate, 78
Regal Chocolate, 78
Shells
Crumb Crust, 35
Meringue Nut Shell, 31
Pie Shell, 35
Souffle Supreme, 56
Sour Cream Topping, 20
Southern Chocolate Pecan Pie, 32
Strawberry Chocolate Mousse, 53
Sweet Coconut Pie, 26

TOPPINGS (See also Fondues,
Frostings, Glazes and Sauces)
Coffee-Flavored, 32
Sour Cream, 20
Truffles, 66
Tutti Frutti Bars, 65
Very Berry Chocolate Cake, 10
Viennese Chocolate Torte, 14
Wellesley Fudge Cake, 12
White-Capped Bars, 73
Yule Log, 22

Design: Wallace/Church Associates, Inc.
Photographed by Victor Scocozza